Victory Over Anger
Rules of Engagement

Endorsements:

*"Life Changing! **Victory Over Anger: Rules of Engagement** saved not only our marriage but our lives."*
—Dwane and Stephanie Montgomery, owners
Dynamite Painting and Remodeling

"A practical and insightful approach in the area of anger management."
—Rev. Jamie L. Storie, MAMFT
Fresh Start Community Church

*"**Victory Over Anger: Rules of Engagement** gave me the tools, words, and knowledge to properly control my anger."*
—Rick Lawrence, retired
Tinker Air Force Base

*"I read **Victory Over Anger: Rules of Engagement** not thinking I had any anger issues. It gently proved me wrong. Years and years of a terrible marriage had taught me to stuff my feelings. This book helped me find constructive and acceptable ways to deal with my feelings before I reached the dreaded explosion most "stuffers" experience. I am happier than I have ever been by learning to accept myself for who I am and by learning I am the one in control!"*
—Stacey Imhoff, customer service specialist
FedEx

"Without this book, I would probably be dead or in prison."
—J.P. Williams, aerospace engineer (civilian)
United States Air Force

*"**Victory Over Anger: Rules of Engagement** taught me that I have power through Christ to choose not to be angry, that I can take control over my anger, gaining a foothold on my thinking. "*

—Sean Gutteridge, worship pastor
Westmoore Community Church

Dr. Teresa Davis, Ed.D.

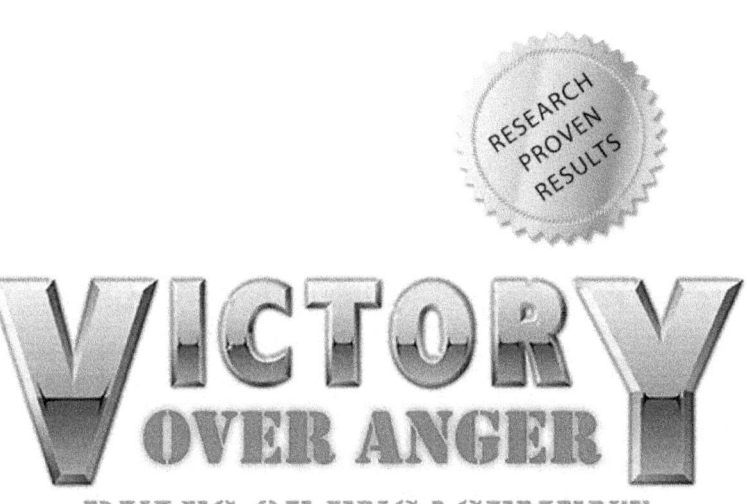

Victory Over Anger: Rules of Engagement
Copyright © 2003, 2018 by Dr. Teresa Davis, Ed.D.
All rights reserved

No part of this publication may be reproduced, stored in a retrieval system or transmitted in any way by any means, electronic, mechanical, photocopy, recording or otherwise without the prior permission of the author except as provided by USA copyright law.

All scripture quotations, unless otherwise indicated, are taken from the Holy Bible, New International Version®.
NIV ® Copyright © 1973, 1978, 1984 by International Bible Society Used by permission of Zondervan. All rights reserved.

Scripture quotations marked (KJV) are taken from the Holy Bible, King James Version, Cambridge, 1769. Used by permission. All rights reserved.

Designed by Brad Davis

ISBN-13: 978-1947121997
ISBN-10: 1947121995

I want to dedicate this book to my husband, Brad, and my two sons, Bradley and Robert. Thank you for loving and forgiving me. Without you, this book would have not been possible.

Special thanks to;

Diane Isam. It was your excitement and encouragement that motivated me to complete this book. Pairing me up with Jessie was a blessing! Thank you so very much!

Jessica Jepson. How can I thank you enough for helping me complete this project? Your words of encouragement have kept me going!

TABLE OF CONTENTS

ENDORSEMENTS:	1
FOREWARD	13
INTRODUCTION	15
CHAPTER 1	21
CHAPTER 2 SELF-TALK	27
CHAPTER 3 OUR THOUGHT PROCESS	33
CHAPTER 4 EMOTIONS AND ANGER	45
CHAPTER 5 REJECTION	51
CHAPTER 6 UNREALISTIC EXPECTATIONS	61
CHAPTER 7 WE WANT OUR WAY	73
CHAPTER 8 ACT OR REACT	81
CHAPTER 9 ARE YOU PASSIVE, AGGRESSIVE, OR ASSERTIVE?	87
CHAPTER 10 SEEING OTHERS' PERSPECTIVES	93
CHAPTER 11 GOAL SETTING	101
CHAPTER 12 ARE YOU ANGRY WITH GOD?	111
CHAPTER 13 FAIR FIGHTING	121
CHAPTER 14 PARENTING AND ANGER	131
CHAPTER 15 TAKING TIME-OUTS	147
CHAPTER 16 ADDITIONAL TOPICS	155
CONCLUSION	167
NOTES TO THE TEXT	171

FOREWARD

As a novelist, I find myself constantly emerged in emotion. By nature, I am a person who is well-acquainted with it, and by trade, I am a writer who must use emotion on the page to evoke it from my readers. Still, is there anything more baffling at times to a human being than their own emotional journey?

Victory Over Anger: Rules of Engagement *by Dr. Teresa Davis has to be one of the most in-depth yet easy to read books on the subject. Oftentimes we don't understand our own emotional journeys, which can lead to a plethora of new emotions emerging that we'd rather not see the light of day. This book helps the reader understand where emotions, such as anger, are birthed, and it is written with such passion and you'll wonder if Dr. Davis has been living inside your soul for the past decade! With firsthand experiences and many other personal stories, she teaches the reader to apply life-changing principles to their own lives.*

My family and I have been personally helped by Dr. Davis's wisdom and her gift for sharing it with her fellow sojourners. She is a warm, delightful woman of God, and you'll see her heart in the pages of this book. More than that, though, I believe God will use this book to help you find the answers you've been searching for and the peace that you're seeking. I can't think of a better person to take you on this journey.

-Rene Gutteridge,
Best selling author of *Never the Bride* and fifteen other Christian fiction novels

INTRODUCTION

I think that it is important for me to start this book by giving you a little history about myself. First and foremost, I am a Christian. I accepted Christ as my Lord and Savior as a very young child and have been involved in church most of my life. I love the Lord with all my heart and for the most part have wanted to live my life by His will, not mine. Sometimes, however, things happen in our lives that we do not understand, and because of this, they could become very difficult to overcome. You see, I am an adult with attention deficit disorder (ADD). I realized I had ADD when I was in my second year of my bachelor's program in a class called *Child and Adolescent Psychology*. One of the topics we discussed in class was children with ADD. I finally understood why I had so many problems as a child. But true reality didn't hit me until several years later when I was working on my master's degree and we had to learn the *Diagnostic and Statistical Manual of Mental Disorders (DSM)* [1]. This is the official diagnostic manual for mental health. As I began to study about

ADD, I wondered if it was a disease that was carried into adulthood. After talking to several people about this, I was referred to a book called *Driven to Distraction, by Doctors Edward M. Hallowell, M.D., and John J. Rately, M.D* [2]. This book unfolded my history before me. I was amazed to read about people who had struggled through life much like I had, with many of the same obstacles to overcome as me.

    I would like to share with you two short paragraphs from *Driven to Distraction*. Not that this book I am writing is about ADD, but it will help you to see how anger was instilled in me as a small child and continued into adulthood. I cried as I read these paragraphs the first time. The reason? Because for the first time in my life I realized why I am like I am. It was a real eye-opener for me.

*   Due to repeated failures, misunderstandings, mislabelings, and all manner of other emotional mishaps, children with ADD usually develop problems with their self-image and self-esteem. Throughout childhood, at home, and at school they are told they are defective. They are called dumb, stupid, lazy, stubborn, willful, or obnoxious. They hear terms like "spaceshot" or "daydreamer" or "out in left field" all the time. They are blamed for the chaos of family mealtimes or the disaster of family vacations. They are reprimanded for classroom disturbances of all sorts and they are easily scapegoated at school. They are the subject of numerous parent-teacher conferences. Time and again, an exasperated teacher meets a frustrated parent in a meeting that later explodes all over the child who isn't there. He feels the shock waves afterward. "Do you know what your teacher said? Do you know how embarrassed your mother and I were?" Or, from the teacher, "I understand you have no greater control of yourself at home than you do in school. We must work on this, mustn't we?"*

Month after month, year after year, the tapes of negativity play over and over again until they become the voice the child knows best. "You're bad," they say in many different ways. "You're dumb. You just don't get it. You're so out of it. You really are pathetic." This voice pulls the child's self-esteem down and down, out of the reach of the helping hands that might be extended, into the private world of adolescent self-reproach. Liking yourself in adolescence is hard enough work for any child. But for the child with ADD it is especially difficult.

It is not difficult to visualize how a child that has experienced what is written in these paragraphs could become an angry individual. You see, I was raised in the sixties and early seventies. There was not a diagnosis of ADD then. I went through a lot of testing in first grade, the same type of test they do today to diagnosis ADD. My parents were told I was hyper, and they were given these little green pills to give me daily. I think they were tranquilizers. I was plenty smart enough—too smart in fact. The solution at the time was to skip me up a grade. Then the work would be harder, and I would stay busier and not get into as much trouble. So I went from first to third grade. The problem was that although I was smart enough to do the work, I was very immature, which is typical for ADD kids.

The older I got, the more problems I experienced due to that immaturity. I remember in the fifth grade I couldn't get along with the kids in my grade, so they made me spend my recess time with the fourth graders. I can still see myself standing alone next to one of the school buildings watching everyone else play while I stayed by myself because I did not know any of the fourth graders.

I cannot tell you how many times I wished I knew what was wrong with me. People would ask me why I did or did not do something, and I would respond with, "*I don't know,*" because I really did not know. I remember feeling more angry as I grew older. When I got into high school, I basically quit trying. The schoolwork took too much concentration, something I didn't have enough of. I got further and further behind. My grades started dropping and I lost interest in school. By the time I was a senior, my grade point average was in the 2.0 range. I believe it was a miracle that I graduated.

By this time, I was angry at school, the teachers, my so-called friends, my parents, and every other person of authority in my life. I just wanted to run away from everything I knew. So, I got married. I was seventeen years old. At first, things were great. Then, as the years went on and as the stress built, I became angrier and angrier. We had two children, whom I adored and never wanted to hurt. But, because of my illness, I didn't know how to be a good mother. I would try really hard, and things would be okay for a while, but then I would explode. It was an endless cycle that I did not know how to break. I think I spanked my older son so much that the skin on his rear became like leather. My husband, Brad, tried to support me the best he could, but without the understanding of the disease I had and the long term effects of that disease, it was very difficult. But Brad stayed with me and put up with my anger. Now, when asked why, he says it was because I had so much hurt in my past that he did not want to add to it.

In 1987, I was twenty-eight years old, and I was miserable. I had been married to a wonderful husband for eleven years. I was involved in my kids' lives as home room mother, soccer coach, and PTA officer. I was a leader at my church, I ran my own successful business from my home, and for the first time in my life, I was finally beginning to build real friendships. But, I did not like who I was. I did not like what was going on inside me. I decided to get some counseling. Through this, I was able to overcome a lot of my past hurts and current problems, but the anger was still there. It wasn't until 1994, when I started my bachelor's program that I began to learn about the roots of my anger and how to overcome the control it had over my life.

So, you see, I am not a person who's just had a little education and decided I could help everyone control his or her anger. No, I have experienced anger firsthand. I was raised in an angry environment; I became angry myself and had to get help to learn how to overcome my inappropriate behavior. I've taught anger management classes, sometimes as many as five times a week, which helped me learn to keep my anger under control. I have spent the last ten years reading, researching, and investigating as much as I can on anger management. From this research, I have developed the information contained in this book.

Anger management is not a skill you learn. It is a life-changing achievement. Once you have read this book and learned to apply the techniques, and you learn and believe the Scripture references used, your life will be changed forever. And it is wonderful. There is such a freedom in having control over your anger instead of your anger having control over you.

The theory I use in counseling and the basic principles of this book are based on cognitive-behavioral therapy. Cognitive is the way we think. Behavioral is the way we act. I believe if I can help you to change the way you think, then the way you act will naturally follow. What we think is based on our history, the way we were raised, the experiences we have encountered, the things we have learned, the choices we have made. What we think is true becomes so much our reality that we sometimes are not willing to see other perspectives. I believe that this is totally in line with scripture. The Bible tells us in 2 Corinthians 5:7 that "*we live by faith not by sight.*" This means that we walk by what we believe (based on what Scripture says) not by what our circumstances look or feel like. We may have been told our whole lives certain negative things that we believe about ourselves. When we apply Scripture, memorize and believe it, we begin to believe what it says instead of what we have been told all of our lives. We use Scripture to change the way we think about ourselves. As we begin to think differently about ourselves, we begin to act differently.

In this book, I will challenge you to reconsider the way you think about things, not to just think and believe things because that is the way you have always known it to be. As you open yourself up to reconsider other ideas and perspectives, you are opening yourself up to the possibility of changing the way you think, therefore ultimately changing the way you act. I hope this information will be as helpful to you as it has been to me.

"Father, I pray today that you would allow this book to minister to the hearts of the individuals reading it. I pray that through your Son, Jesus Christ, you will melt the hardness that has built around their hearts as they read, process, and learn the applications and techniques taught. Lord, it is amazing to me that you would come down from your throne to care for each one of our individual needs. You care about every detail of our lives. I pray that you would help us to become the people that you originally created us to be. Show us the areas that we need to change, and then teach us how to change them. Draw us near to you, Father, so we can become more like you. In the most precious name of your Son, Jesus. Amen."

CHAPTER 1
Anger Is a Choice

The first and probably the most important thing we must learn about anger is that our display of it, or how we deal with it, is our choice. We have a tendency to say, "*You make me...*" whatever it is we feel. We blame others for our feelings. In actuality, what can anyone really "*make*" you do? Nothing! Right?

We as human beings can choose to be or not to be offended when someone says something offensive to us. The problem is that most people don't realize this. They think that if someone offends them, they are supposed to get their feelings hurt. They think it is justified to get angry about it. But reality is, when someone does something offensive, we choose whether or not we want to be offended and then act accordingly.

As parents, we tend to blame our children for our anger, saying things like, "*You make me so mad,*" or "*You make me angry.*" Then, later down the line, our children do something naughty and we ask them, "*Why did you do that?*" A child's typical response to that question can be, "*He made me do it.*" Then we punish them for blaming others, but from whom did they learn how to blame in the first place? Us!

We live in a world of blame. We say things like, "*That makes me mad,*" "*This makes me happy,*" and "*You make me sad.*" All our lives we have blamed our feelings on others instead of taking responsibility for them ourselves.

We can change blame to responsibility just by changing a couple of words. Instead of saying "*You make me feel...*" begin to say "*I feel*" or "*I choose to feel.*" As we begin to retrain our way of speaking, we will retrain our way of thinking. When we realize that we choose to be angry, we also realize that we can choose to not be angry. Many people come to anger management wanting to get rid of their anger completely. This is impossible. Anger is a God-given emotion that we need in order to survive in this world. We use anger for protection, in cases of injustice, and other areas of our life. If someone is breaking into our home, we need anger to help us protect ourselves. If someone abuses us, we need anger to help fight the abuse. If we see an injustice being done to us or to someone else, anger will help us fight against the injustice. Our goal should be to learn to handle anger appropriately instead of eliminating it.

The Bible tells us that it is okay to be angry as long as we do not sin. Psalm 4:4 says, "*In your anger do not sin; when you are on your beds, search your hearts and be silent.*" When you are angry, you should go to a quiet place and examine your heart to find out what is really angering you. Then choose an acceptable way to express the way you are feeling. Ephesians 4:26–27 says, "*In your anger do not sin: Do not let the sun go down while you are still angry, and do not give the devil a foothold.*" If we sin while we are angry, by displaying the anger in inappropriate ways, we allow the devil a foothold in our lives. Gossip is sin[1]. If we talk to others about what another person has done to us, and those people are not in a position to help the situation, that is called gossip. If we mope around while we are angry, wanting someone to pay attention to us, instead of being honest and discussing the matter with the person involved, we are sinning[2]. When we are angry and we deal with that anger in an unacceptable way (according to the Word), we are sinning. Remember, the scripture says, *"In your anger, do not sin."*

It says in 1 Peter 3:12, *"For the eyes of the Lord are on the righteous and his ears are attentive to their prayer, but the face of the Lord is against those who do evil."* Psalm 24:3–4 says, *"Who may ascend the hill of the LORD? Who may stand in his holy place? He who has clean hands and a pure heart."* When we have sin in our lives, it causes a separation between God and us. If there is a separation between God and us, then the enemy has a greater opportunity to cause havoc in our lives and somehow convince us to sin even more.

Everyone experiences anger to some extent; therefore, anger management is for everyone. Many people say they don't yell, scream, or hit, so they don't feel like they need anger management. I hear this a lot from clients who are court ordered to take an anger management class. Many times the people who say this are people who suppress or stuff their anger instead of releasing it. Stuffing anger is just as inappropriate as expressing anger in an external way, and it is actually physically harder on the person stuffing. People who suppress their anger are actually like a volcano that can erupt any time, any place. Hiding anger is hard on a person's physical body because God did not make our bodies to hold anger in. If the anger is held in long enough, the physical body starts breaking down from the internal stress. Individuals who stuff their anger experience heart problems, stomach problems, headaches, intestinal problems, and many more physical ailments from the pressure they are holding inside. The truth is that everyone needs to learn to appropriately control the anger they have. If they don't, the anger will creep out, usually at the most inopportune times.

In one of my men's anger management classes, I had a client who stated he never yelled or screamed and rarely even got upset. He stated that he was pretty much a passive person and things usually didn't get to him. When asked why he was court ordered to the class, he replied that he was in a custody battle with his ex-wife. He currently had full custody of his three boys, and his wife was trying to take that from him. During his last court appearance, his wife began to tell outrageous lies about him to the judge. He said he listened quietly as long as he could, but his wife just kept lying until he couldn't take it anymore and he blew up. This not only got him court ordered to anger management class, but it also cost him custody of his boys until he completed the class.

I hear stories like this quite often. People who claim to not have an anger problem, but one time they blew up, at the wrong time, in front of the wrong person, and it cost them. This is why it is important for everyone to learn how to handle the anger they do have in appropriate ways. Then, when things do get difficult, when stress rises, when a person has taken all they can take, they will be able to choose to handle their anger correctly.

Most of my life, people told me to control my anger. My kids and my husband asked me time and again not to yell. I would respond by saying something like *"I'm not yelling"* or *"I can't help it."* I realized one day that when I was yelling my head off and the phone rang or someone rang the doorbell, I could suddenly stop yelling and could act quite normal to the other people. Then as soon as I hung up the phone or closed the door, I picked right up where I left off. I realized that if I could stop yelling for other people, I should be able to stop yelling at my family; as a matter of fact, I should be able to stop yelling altogether. Have you ever realized that we are the nicest to friends and visitors and the meanest to our family? Shouldn't that be the other way around?

Anger is a choice. We can choose to be angry or not to be angry. We can choose to act our anger out appropriately or inappropriately. We can choose to not be offended. The choices we make are up to us. We need to stop blaming others for the way we feel and act, and take responsibility for our own actions.

CHAPTER 2
Self-Talk

Self-talk is what you do when you find yourself in a situation and are not sure how to act correctly. I decided a while back that if I could teach all my clients to use positive self-talk instead of negative self-talk, I could teach myself right out of a job. If we will take the time, we can positively self-talk ourselves through anything.

Let me give you an example of positive self-talk. One time, one of my dear friends said something to me that at first was very offensive. I stopped myself from reacting and did some self-talk. I told myself that this was one of my friends, and I knew she loved me very much. I knew she would never do anything to purposely hurt me. I told myself that she probably did not even realize what she had just said. Then I was able to choose not to be insulted by what she said.

You see, most of what we take as offensive is only our perception. Even though it is true that our perception is our reality, we can choose to look at the other person's perspective or look at the reality of the situation instead of what it seems or feels like, and we can overcome what would typically be an undesirable response. What we automatically feel is not necessarily the truth. Sometimes we have to actually list facts in our heads—self-talk—in order to see the situation differently. That is just what I did with this friend. I listed to myself what I knew to be facts about this friend. When I was able to do that, I was able not to take offense at what she had said.

We can do this same thing in many situations. Countless arguments are caused by a lack of understanding of what the other person is saying. In anger, we tend to say things in a way that doesn't always come across as nice. Also, in anger, we perceive things worse than they really are. Evaluating the situation before responding can calm a potentially dangerous argument. This is especially true with spouses. I have been married more than forty two years. I know Brad pretty well by now. Sometimes he says some pretty ridiculous things that I could really get upset about. But, when I take my time and evaluate him and what was just said, I can keep myself from reacting to what he says. Just as with the friend I mentioned earlier, I know Brad loves me and he doesn't say things to purposely hurt me. Sometimes he just doesn't think before he speaks. Isn't it all right to give him a break sometimes? I know I say a lot of things I shouldn't say. I have a tendency to open my mouth to insert my foot. Since I unknowingly say things that hurt others, shouldn't I have more grace for others when they do the same thing? We are inclined to be critical toward characteristics we don't like in other people, because they are the same characteristics we don't like about ourselves.

Sometimes when my husband says something that at first seems insulting, I will ask him what he meant before I react. I will tell him that what I just perceived him to say was mean, insulting, harsh, offensive, or that I felt hurt. Since his intention isn't to offend me or to hurt my feelings, he will think about what he just said and then apologize for hurting my feelings or offending me. Then he will think about a more appropriate way to reword what he was trying to say. Many times this will help us both to communicate better with each other instead of fighting about what we thought the other just said. Haven't you gotten in plenty of arguments where you end up saying, *"but you said..."* and the other person says, *"That's not what I said,"* then another argument ensues about that? It is all because of a lack of understanding about what the other person was trying to say.

For some reason, we have a tendency to perceive everything as negative, especially in arguments, even in the simplest little things. I can ask Brad if he did something, and his first reaction is to think I am criticizing him. I could have been planning to compliment him on the job he did, but he hasn't given me the chance because he jumps on me for criticizing him. This is where self-talk comes in. Brad can tell himself to wait before reacting to see where I am going with this conversation. He can tell himself to calm down and not to perceive the negative until he knows for sure what I am trying to say.

Using scripture as self-talk is very valuable. If we are having negative feelings about ourselves, we can begin to confess scripture that is contrary to what we are feeling.

"I am the righteousness of God in Christ Jesus." [1]
"I can do all things through Jesus Christ who gives me strength." [2]
"God works all things together for good for me because I love Him and am called according to His purpose." [3]

These scriptures are positive affirmations we can say to ourselves to counteract the negative way we are feeling. We can also tell ourselves,

"I have an abundant life because of Jesus." [4]
"I am a child of God in Christ Jesus." [5]
"I am more than a conqueror through Christ." [6]

The enemy cannot stand to hear the Word of God quoted to him. The more scripture we memorize, the more we have on hand to quote, and the more effective we are against the negative thoughts the enemy puts into our heads.

When we are dealing with a difficult situation that we have turned over to God, we can self-talk ourselves out of taking it back from Him. The enemy will try to get you to dwell on the situation, even worry about it. When you find yourself worrying or thinking again about something you have prayed and asked God to handle, say things to yourself like, *"This isn't my thing. I have already given this to God. I am not taking it back. I am not going to worry about this. Worrying doesn't change things. Worrying about this will only take it back from God. Worry is sin. I will not sin on purpose."* Saying these things to yourself over and over will help you to overcome the urge to worry or dwell on the situation. You can also talk to the enemy. *"You are not going to get me to worry about this situation. This is none of your business. I will not fall into your trap. I rebuke you in Jesus' name."* Then try to begin to think of something good. Try to think of something really fun you have recently done or something you are looking forward to. Think about something funny that has happened. Think about how much you love your spouse, your kids, or your grandkids. Think about all the wonderful things God has done for you in your life. When you counter the negative thoughts with positive ones, the negative ones will cease.

I tend to be the type of person who reacts immediately instead of thinking through things. Self-talk has helped me learn to wait before responding. I'll give you an example. One time during a church service, I looked toward the back and saw that my youngest son was no longer sitting with his friends in the youth group. I instantly became angry with him because he knew he was not allowed to leave in the middle of a church service. From that point on, I remember nothing of what my pastor was saying. I was consumed by thoughts of what I was going to do to him after church. I kept looking toward the back to see if he had returned. I figured he and his girlfriend were in the youth room, outside, or walking the halls instead of being in church. By the time service was over, I was an angry mess. I searched the church for him and couldn't find him. I looked in the parking lot, and his car was gone. Boy, was he in trouble. I became angrier and angrier during our drive home. Because I was so angry, my husband got it too. I yelled and screamed the whole way about what "*his*" son had done and how unhappy I was about it.

Since I had already determined that he was out goofing off, I was a bit surprised to find that his car was parked in the driveway when I got home. I jumped out of the car (probably while it was still moving) and ran into the house. I went straight to his room, yelling before I even reached him. I opened his door to find him sprawled out on his bed, white as a ghost. In the process of me yelling, I somehow asked him who he thought he was to get up and leave in the middle of church. In a weak, moaning voice, he said to me, *"Mama, I'm really sick. I started throwing up in church. I didn't want to walk to the front of the church to tell you I was leaving, so I just left."*

Whew! What a slap in the face that was for me. I had just ruined my and my husband's morning, missed what was probably a very good sermon, and may have made a fool of myself at the church, without even giving my son the chance to explain why he had left. Man, did I feel like an idiot! I apologized to my son and went into my room and lay on my bed. The Lord instantly convicted me of not only losing my temper, but of unjust anger. I had to make a determination at that point that I would wait until I had all the details before responding to any situation.

I am not perfect by any means, but self-talk has helped me to overcome that ingrained way of responding to what I at first perceive as unwanted or negative situations. I can say to myself, *"Hold on now. Don't react. Wait a minute. Breathe. I don't know all the details. Keep calm."* Not only does talking to myself keep me from inappropriate outbursts of anger, but it also helps me to be in control when I do find out that what I assumed was accurate and this is a time for righteous, appropriate, anger. Remember, it is normal and healthy to feel anger. It is not normal or right to act out that anger in inappropriate ways.

Self-talk can save us from a lot of embarrassing moments. If we react before thinking (and self-talking) in public and around family or friends, we can really say and do some dumb stuff. The more we learn to self-talk, the more we will find ourselves acting appropriate and feeling less embarrassed.

CHAPTER 3
Our Thought Process

What we think about can control the way we act, who we are, our attitudes, and our outlook on life. Our thoughts have the power to form who we are to become. If we consistently think negative thoughts, we will be negative people. If we consistently think positive thoughts, we will live a more positive life. People with negative attitudes tend to be angry people, but not many people with positive attitudes are angry people. The Bible tells us in Philippians 4:8,

"Whatever is true, whatever is noble, whatever is right, whatever is pure, whatever is lovely, whatever is admirable—if anything is excellent or praiseworthy—think about such things."

I used to stay home during the day while Brad was at work and the boys were at school. I would think about something one of them had done that I hadn't necessarily liked, and I would start getting angry about it. I would begin thinking of other things that had happened in the past that I had also gotten angry about but never really dealt with. The more I thought about it, the angrier I would become. I would determine that we would discuss it as soon as they got home. I discussed it okay—the minute they would walk through the door, I would blast them. I would rant and rave about all kinds of stuff, even things that didn't pertain to what I had originally gotten angry about. All this because of one thing I chose to dwell on too long.

The enemy wants to cause division between people. In Matthew 13:38–39, we are told that weeds that are planted are *"the sons of the evil one, and the enemy who sows them is the devil."*[1] Negative thoughts are weeds sown into our minds by the enemy. As a result, we become angry with the people we are thinking about. If the enemy can cause families, friends, and all sorts of other relationships to become angry enough at each other, they will divide, or separate from one another. This can start as a result of one thought. Then one thought builds on another thought, then another and another. We can take ownership of those thoughts and believe them to be true, or recognize them as coming from the enemy and rebuke them.

My poor family, I was so mean to them. Brad told me one time that he would worry all the way home from work about what kind of a mood I would be in when he got there and what I would be angry about. Wouldn't it be awful to live like that? Thank God that He cared enough about me and my family to convict me of these things then help me to overcome them. The Bible tells us in 2 Corinthians 10:4–5 that:

The weapons we fight with are not the weapons of the world. On the contrary, they have divine power to demolish strongholds. We demolish arguments and every pretension that sets itself up against the knowledge of God, and we take captive every thought to make it obedient to Christ.

Paul is telling us here that we have been given the weapons we need to defeat all those negative thoughts.

Ephesians 6:13–18 tells us what those weapons are—battle armor. Verse 17 says the sword of the Spirit is the Word of God[2]. We can use the Word of God to combat the negative thoughts that are constantly being driven into our minds. Let's discuss how this works.

Looking back, the first time I remember that major changes were being made in my life was after I started studying the Word of God the first thing every day. I would refresh my mind with the good things in the Word instead of the negative things the devil wanted to put in there. There were several years that I spent hours studying every morning. Then, when I would go to my machine to sew (I had a sewing business in my home when my boys were young), I would put on praise music or preaching tapes. This would help me stay focused on positive thoughts instead of negative ones; plus, I was learning something good in the process.

Since we didn't have much money, I asked friends of mine to bring me preaching tapes from their churches. I would have the sound person at my church give me copies of tapes they made during worship. I built up quite a library of things to listen to over the years. I still do this today. When I am feeling down or negative, I will find an old tape and listen to it. Actually, I have continued over the years to purchase different tape series from pastors and evangelists who I have heard on TV or radio. I constantly go online to purchase and download the newest worship music and sermon podcasts. I love to keep positive things going into my mind. I don't want the enemy to dwell there. Now Brad can look forward to coming home to be with me without being concerned about how angry I will be when he gets there.

Many people think it is too difficult to think positively instead of negatively, but the truth is that they both take equal amounts of energy. The reason the negative seems so much easier is because it is habit. For most, habits are hard to break. It takes practice. But everything you do in life that you want to do well takes practice. Whether it is sports, music, cooking, art, or playing video games, it takes practice to be good at them. Even the most famous people have to continue to practice what they do to remain in the spotlight. The same is true with the negative things in life. For example: Do you practice complaining? If your answer is yes, then I bet you are really good at it. Whatever you do on a consistent basis becomes who you are. The more you practice, the better you become at it. If you practice dwelling on negative thoughts, then you will be really good at being a negative person. When you practice being angry as a result, you will be really angry. When put into that perspective, it doesn't sound very good, does it?

I will probably say this next statement, or ones similar to it, several times in this book, because it is one that is very important to remember when dealing with anger. It isn't the situation itself, but how we perceive that situation, that makes the difference. Is my cup half-full or half-empty? I have developed the chart on the following page to help you understand that the way we perceive a situation and apply scripture to it really does make a difference.

VICTORY OVER ANGER

A THE ACTUAL EVENT ⇨ B BELIEF ABOUT THE EVENT ⇨ C CONSEQUENCES, THE WAY YOU FEEL
⇩
D DISPUTING INTERVENTION ⇨ E EFFECT ⇨F NEW FEELING
(applying scripture) (changes that take place) (based on what you know scripture says)

Example:

A (actual event) = "I'll never get a job."
B (belief) = "I am a failure."
C (consequences) = Depression & Hopelessness
D (dispute) = "I can do everything through Him who gives me strength." (Phil. 4:13)
   "My God will meet all your needs according to His glorious riches in Christ Jesus" (Phil. 4:19)
E (effect) = "I will find a job."
F (feeling) = No longer depressed, but optimistic and hopeful.

Isaiah 55:11 says, *"So is my word that goes out from my mouth: It will not return to me empty, but will accomplish what I desire and achieve the purpose for which I sent it."* When we memorize God's Word, then confess it with our mouths, we are sending it out. God says it will not come back to Him empty but will do what He sent it to do. As we confess scripture, we are building our faith about what those scriptures are saying. And the more we confess scripture over our lives and situations, the more God will be working to accomplish those promises for us.

Meditating on God's Word is another way to keep your thoughts positive instead of negative. Webster's Dictionary[3] defines meditate as *"to focus one's thoughts on."* Several writers of the Old Testament discuss meditating on God's words. God told Joshua and the people of Israel, *"Do not let this Book of the Law depart from your mouth; meditate on it day and night, so that you may be careful to do everything written in it. Then you will be prosperous and successful "* (Joshua 1:8). Then the psalmist gives us a beautiful description of what happens when we meditate on God's law (the Word) as in *Psalm 119:97–105;*

"Oh, how I love your law! I meditate on it all day long. Your commands make me wiser than my enemies, for they are ever with me. I have more insight than all my teachers, for I meditate on your statutes. I have more understanding than the elders, for I obey your precepts. I have kept my feet from every evil path so that I might obey your word. I have not departed from your laws, for you yourself have taught me. How sweet are your words to my taste, sweeter than honey to my mouth! I gain understanding from your precepts; therefore I hate every wrong path. Your word is a lamp to my feet and a light for my path."

Besides helping us to not focus on negative thoughts, meditating on God's Word can be effective in many other areas of our lives such as prosperity and success, and it gives us wisdom and understanding.

The Bible also tells us in Matthew 12:34, "*out of the overflow of the heart the mouth speaks.*" Whatever is in our hearts will come out of our mouths. If we have a lot of negative, unresolved garbage in our hearts, it will taint everything that comes out of our mouths in a negative way. Then everything we say will sound as if it is coming from an angry person. Remember the old saying, "*Garbage in, garbage out* "? It isn't necessarily something we plan or intend to do. It just happens. It could be from things that happened to us as a kid, like it was with me. I was a totally negative person.

To be honest, negativity is still one of the major issues I find myself struggling with today. When it seems your whole life is full of negative things (as it was with me when I was young), it is very difficult to not be negative. It is only by the grace of God, and His Word, that I am where I am today. I can usually catch myself if I begin to talk in the negative. I have close friends who will confront me instead of joining my pity party. And I have so much Word in me that there just isn't much room left in my little heart for the negative to stay. When we fill our hearts with the Word, the Word will come out of our mouths. I'm not saying that you will be quoting scripture all the time. But just as the negative in your heart will taint the words that come out of your mouth, the Word (or positive) in your heart will purify the words that come out of your mouth.

Another area that can cause you to have negative thoughts is worry. I have had several great discussions about worry with men of faith. My belief is that worry is sin. The New Testament quotes Jesus as saying, "*do not worry*" eleven times. To me, that alone, is significant. I believe that anything the Bible specifically tells us not to do, but we choose to do it anyway, is sin. (Anything done without faith is sin. Hebrews 11:6.) Read the following quote taken from Luke 12:22–32. It is a long quote, but I think it very compelling when considering the topic of worry. Then Jesus said to His disciples:

> *"Therefore I tell you, do not worry about your life, what you will eat; or about your body, what you will wear. Life is more than food, and the body more than clothes. Consider the ravens: They do not sow or reap, they have no storeroom or barn; yet God feeds them. And how much more valuable you are than birds! Who of you by worrying can add a single hour to his life? Since you cannot do this very little thing, why do you worry about the rest? Consider how the lilies grow. They do not labor or spin. Yet I tell you, not even Solomon in all his splendor was dressed like one of these. If that is how God clothes the grass of the field, which is here today, and tomorrow is thrown into the fire, how much more will He clothe you, O you of little faith! And do not set your heart on what you will eat or drink; do not worry about it. For the pagan world runs after all such things, and your Father knows that you need them. But seek His kingdom, and these things will be given to you as well. Do not be afraid, little flock, for your Father has been pleased to give you the kingdom."*

The Lord goes into such detail here about how much He loves us and how He wants to care for us. He instructs us to seek Him instead of worrying. We do that by self-talk and confessing promises like these from the scriptures. If we continue to worry, we not only sin, but we can allow that worry to control our thoughts. Then we can become angry because the situation isn't going the way we think it should, or because God isn't doing what we think He should be doing about it.

I used to be the world's greatest worrier. I worried all the time about the stupidest stuff. I worried so much it literally made me sick. The Lord convicted me of this one night as I lay in bed worrying about my kids. They had spent the day at the lake with some friends. They came home all excited about the fun they had. They gave me all the details about their activities of the day. On the outside, I was rejoicing with them. But on the inside I was falling apart. Why? Because I was so dimwitted, I worried about what *"could have"* happened to them. I couldn't sleep that night because I worried about it so much. I kept picturing in my mind different things that could have happened to them while they were riding on the wave runners or diving off cliffs.

I heard the Lord quietly ask me, *"What are you doing?"* I was startled for a second and didn't reply. He repeated the question, *"What are you doing?"* Not understanding, I still didn't reply. The Lord, being so sweet and understanding, showed me exactly what I was doing. He showed me that my kids were at home with me, safe, and sleeping in their own beds. The day was over, and nothing bad had happened. Then He asked me, *"Why are you worrying about something that is past? You can't change anything by worrying about it."* I responded by telling Him that I didn't know why I was doing it but that I couldn't help it. I couldn't just make myself stop worrying. He told me to stop myself by thinking of something else that was better. He told me to force my mind to dwell on something good, like how happy the kids were when they got home. He told me to focus on their smiling faces and twinkling eyes as they spoke of how much fun they had had. So I tried it, and each time I would begin to drift back to the worry, I would feel him nudge me back to pleasant thoughts again. This was my first experience with self-talk, and I wasn't even in school yet. It was a lesson straight from God.

The Lord showed me that there are three major things in life that we worry about; things that have happened (and we can't change them), things that might happen, and the things we are currently involved in. When we are worrying about any of these things, we are not trusting in him. The scripture earlier mentioned, Hebrews 11:6, tells us, *"And without faith it is impossible to please God, because anyone who comes to Him must believe that He exists and that He rewards those who earnestly seek Him"*. Worry is the opposite of faith. Without faith, we cannot please God. This scripture tells us it is impossible. How can we worry about things and at the same time believe that He is going to reward us?

Whenever you catch yourself worrying, try to refocus. Think about something good that has happened. The more you practice doing this, the better you will become. You will be surprised at how much you can stop yourself from worrying by making this simple adjustment. There are times when the things in my mind are so overwhelming that I cannot force myself to change my focus. This can be as a result of my own tendency to worry, because of the ADD, because I am sick or tired or stressed, or because the enemy is attacking really hard. In any case, my only alternative is to pray. Second Corinthians 12:9 says that Christ's strength is made perfect in our weaknesses[4]. The things I cannot accomplish in my own strength can be accomplished through the strength of God. Philippians 4:13 says, *"I can do everything through Him who gives me strength,"* and Matthew 19:26 says, *"With man this is impossible, but with God all things are possible."* No matter what the circumstance, when I feel weak, I can pray and ask God to help me refocus my thoughts. I confess to Him the promises of His Word, and He always sees me through. I have to do my part—that is pray and have faith. I rebuke the enemy and his thoughts. Then I can trust God to take care of it.

A good way to think of the process of controlling our thoughts is to think, "I will control my thoughts. I will not let my thoughts control me." Do you remember the story in the Bible about the woman with the issue of blood? She had spent twelve years of her life and all her money trying to get healed. When she heard that Jesus was coming her way, the scripture tells us, "*she thought, 'If I just touch His clothes, I will be healed'* (Mark 5:28). She did not allow her past or her present circumstances to control her thoughts. She just knew in her heart that if she were able to touch the hem of His garment, she would be healed. Her healing came as a result of a single thought. She controlled her thoughts that day. Her thoughts did not control her.

We are told in Acts 8 that Peter cursed a man because he "*thought*" he could buy the gift of God with money (verse 20).[5]

In these two simple stories, we can see how our thoughts can bless or curse us. In the same way, our thoughts can help us choose whether or not we are going to get angry. It is all based on what you do once that first thought enters your mind. Try it and see. I think you will be pleasantly surprised.

CHAPTER 4
Emotions and Anger

As a whole, our society tends to only express the emotion of anger. In reality, there is usually one or more other emotions involved in any given situation, but the one that is usually expressed is anger. Let's discuss why.

When our little boys come into the house crying because they have fallen down, we tell them to tough it out, not to cry because boys don't cry. We tell each of them to "*be a man.*" When our little girls come in crying because a friend calls them names, we tell them they will make up soon, that the friend didn't mean it, or to just go play. We don't validate our children's feelings. Many parents do not know how to express anger in appropriate ways, so our children hear us yelling and screaming or, maybe worse, hitting (I'm not talking about appropriate spanking for punishment). What have we taught our children? We have taught them that it is not okay to express our real emotions of being hurt, sad, or unhappy, but it is okay to show anger. So, our children grow up stuffing their true emotions and expressing anger instead. This is usually done in improper ways.

Here is an example of how we tend to express anger in place of all the other emotions. Let's say you are driving down the street with your children in the backseat of the car. Suddenly another car comes out of nowhere and hits you in the side of the car where your children are sitting. After making sure they are okay, you jump out of your car yelling and screaming at the idiot who just hit you. What emotion do you think you felt right before the anger kicked in? It may have been for only a fraction of a second, or it may stay with you, but you chose to express the anger instead, mostly out of habit. Did you guess fear? If you did you were right. Parents will quickly experience fear when they feel the lives of their children are threatened. It is a natural emotion. But anger can quickly take over, and the fear is never expressed.

Another example of anger expressed in place of a true emotion is in the case of a death of a close loved one. Many people will only express anger about the death, and often they express it at others they love, causing additional hurt to friends and family. They never express sadness or grief over the loss of their loved one. Usually, it is because they don't know how. In other words, they take their hurt from the loss out on others in the form of anger. This happened to me when I was in my early teens. My aunt, whom my father loved very much, died at a young age. My dad did not know how to handle the hurt he was feeling, so he expressed anger. He said some awful things during this time, which hurt me and other members of our family. Sometimes, when hurtful things are expressed during stressful times, they hurt worse and stay longer. I still remember my dad telling me during that time that if it weren't for me, our family would not have any problems. At that moment he placed all the blame for our family problems on me. It took me years of carrying that around and believing it before I came to the understanding that he was speaking out of hurt and did not realize what he had said.

Any emotion that is not expressed and/or validated is usually suppressed. Suppressed anger is anger that has been stuffed down inside a person instead of it being expressed outward. Eventually, all those stuffed feelings will surface. This can happen in two ways: explosion or implosion. When we explode it is an outward expression of our anger. Usually, an explosion includes uncontrolled violent and/or abusive actions toward others. This is emotionally exhausting for those of us doing it, and then we add to that the feelings of guilt we experience afterwards.

Think of a bomb, the way it blows everything out. Remember the bombing of the Murrah Federal Building in downtown Oklahoma City on April 19, 1995? Television screens across the world showed pictures of a building that the insides had basically been blown out of, along with several surrounding buildings being damaged from the blast. This is what happens when we explode. We let out all that has been building up inside of us, and the blast from us usually hurts others who are around us when we blow. An implosion is the opposite; everything is blown inward. It is when we get angry about something, but instead of releasing that anger, we hold it in. Remember when they imploded the Murrah Federal Building after the initial bombing? The engineers were able to set the dynamite so that when it blew, it caused everything to fall inward, so the surrounding buildings weren't damaged more. When we implode, we shove everything inside. This causes all kinds of physical and mental stress. Our bodies are not equipped to handle implosions. The anger will come out in another form like aches and pains or emotional overloads.

Here is an illustration to help you better understand what can happen when emotions are not dealt with properly.

Imagine a clear pond in the middle of the field. The pond is clean with nothing floating around in it. It is a beautiful summer afternoon, a cool breeze blowing, but not enough to stir up the water. Suddenly there comes one of those Oklahoma summer rains—the kind that come up quickly and violently. The water is abruptly turned and tossed by strong winds. As you again look across the pond you now see a lot of trash and rubble floating around in it. This is all the stuff that has been blown into the pond during the years and has settled to the bottom over time. Now the storm has stirred up the water and caused all the junk to float to the top.

This is what happens with emotional things that happen in our lives that are not dealt with. They sink to the bottom for a time. But as soon as the storms of life come up (and they will), all the junk from the past that was ignored, stuffed, or shoved out of our minds comes back to the surface. We are then forced to deal with them or shove them down again, adding to the existing pile of problems we are facing. This can go on for a lifetime, putting our physical health at risk, as well as our mental, psychological, and emotional health.

The correct thing to do with feelings is to learn how to express them instead of stuffing them. This is a difficult process, especially for men, because, as we all know, *"Men are not supposed to talk about emotions."* I heard that all my life and believed it until I became a counselor. It didn't take very many counseling sessions with men to learn that it wasn't that they didn't want to talk about what they were feeling, or that they weren't supposed to, but that they didn't know how. Most men are very confused about what their true feelings are. No one has taken the time to teach them. So it is passed on from generation to generation that men don't talk about emotions. Once they are taught how and are given the chance, men can talk about what they are feeling just as well as women, and it doesn't cause them to feel less masculine. Actually, it helps them to feel better about themselves because they understand themselves better.

One basic anger management skill is recognizing when we begin to feel the emotion of anger coming on. As we learn to recognize within us what that beginning stage feels like, we can then deal with the matter in a more acceptable manner. We do this through the process of self-talk, which is discussed in Chapter 2. Some questions to ask yourself are: What is the real emotion I am feeling here? How can I express the true emotion of this situation in an appropriate way? How can I stop myself from expressing anger instead?

Questions like these will help you slow down the process of anger outbursts and/or suppressions. It is in times like this that you can take a few minutes to yourself before reacting to a situation. These moments to oneself are called "*time-outs.*" You may even have to tell the person you are with at the time a situation occurs that you need to take a time-out so you can think for a few moments before responding. For more information, read Chapter 15 in this book called "*Taking Time-Outs.*"

CHAPTER 5
Rejection

Rejection can be instilled in us at any age, through traumatic events such as abuse, abandonment, and embarrassment, but also through seemingly "harmless" things like teasing and joking. One or more of these negative occurrences added on can escalate the feelings of rejection. We subconsciously begin to base much of what we say or do on avoiding these feelings. It is very important to note here a frequently used counseling slogan: "A person's perception is their reality." Sometimes the feeling of rejection stems only from how we look at a situation. For example, you see two people having a discussion, and one of them glances your way for a second. You think they are talking about you, and immediately you feel rejected. The reality is that they may not have been talking about you at all. Feelings of rejection are real to the person feeling it—even if the rejection is imagined.

Let me tell you a story about a boy named Nathan who went to kindergarten for the first time. After school, he ran to his parent and said he never wanted to go back. Somebody in his class made fun of him because he wore glasses. The parent, knowing Nathan had to go back to school, tried to distract him or make him think it wasn't so bad. They might say something like, *"That's just stupid. You have to go to school,"* and just leave it as at that. So Nathan went back to school the next day, and the same thing happened. He was teased every day when he went to school. This little boy was feeling more and more rejected. He didn't know how to deal with these feelings, so he would usually cope in one of two ways: He would withdraw to himself or become the class bully. Both of these characteristics were built on a low self-esteem. Nathan did not feel good about himself. If Nathan was also experiencing abuse at home, or if he was living in a one-parent home, the feelings of rejection would likely increase.

Abuse of any kind will add to feelings of rejection because the person being abused feels rejected by the person doing the abusing. When a child is raised in a single-parent home, especially if the other parent is not actively involved in the child's life, he will experience feelings of rejection because the child feels that the parent who isn't there is rejecting him. This is also true when the child is adopted or there is a stepparent involved. No matter how hard you try, there is no one that can replace a biological parent in a child's life. We don't usually hear of children or adults who wonder why their grandparents, aunts, uncles, etc., didn't want them. It is always, *"Why didn't my mother and/or father want me?"*

So Nathan, who had been teased, abused, abandoned, and/or embarrassed, had ingrained within him a deep root of rejection. As he matured, he naturally began to learn to cope with those feelings. His ways of coping would include behaviors that prevent him from feeling rejected. Many of these behaviors would become unhealthy habits. He might become a people pleaser, thinking that if he was able to make everyone happy, then no one would reject him. He might become a perfectionist, thinking that if everything in his whole life was perfect, then there wouldn't be anything for people to reject. As mentioned before, he might become the class bully. As he got older, he might get into more and more fights. As an adult he would then act like the "*big tough guy,*" so that everyone would be impressed. If people were impressed enough by this, they wouldn't reject him. Many teenagers who struggle with the fear of rejection will begin to use drugs and/or drink alcohol. They give into peer pressure. They think that if they are doing what their peers are doing they won't be rejected. All of these "*ways of coping*" are unhealthy. Nathan has grown into an adult who is very insecure and has low self-esteem. He is living his life the way he has trained himself through coping with rejection.

    If you can relate to any of this, you probably struggle with the fear of rejection. Everyone, at some time or another in his or her life, has felt rejected. The feelings and fear of rejection are normal until they become so strong that they consume our every movement and word. Many people never realize that it is rejection, or the fear of it, that motivates their unhealthy actions. The person who is the perfectionist has no idea that the fear of rejection is what motivated him into becoming the person he is. I know this because I was a perfectionist myself. I never knew that being such could be unhealthy. I thought it was a good thing because my life was always in order. What I didn't realize was that, because of my perfectionism, I was causing misery to everyone in my life. You see, I not only wanted perfection in my life, I wanted my husband and my kids to be perfect to; this way they would not be a negative reflection of me. Again, I was avoiding rejection.

It is incredible the way the Lord walked me through the process of recognizing and overcoming the fear of rejection in my life. I was in the second year of my master's program. We were studying about obsessive-compulsive disorders. Just so you will know, obsessive deals with the mind, compulsive deals with the action. A person that struggles with obsessive-compulsive disorder "*thinks*" something bad will happen if they don't "*do*" a certain thing. This is the type of person who has to wash their hands five times in a row with a new bar of soap or "*they will get dangerous germs and die.*" Washing their hands over and over is the compulsive part; their fear of consequences if they don't is the obsessive part. As we began to study about being compulsive, I felt a little alarm go off inside of me. I asked a few questions during our discussion time, and I realized that I had a tendency to be compulsive. My professor told us that being compulsive isn't necessarily bad. It is only bad when it consistently interrupts your normal activities. I thought about what he said for a while and decided I needed to discuss this with my advisor, so I made an appointment to go see her.

During the same time frame that this was going on, I began to cry out to God to help me overcome some other feelings I was having. I would go to church every week with high expectations of what I was going to receive when I got there. I looked forward to seeing my friends, worship, and learning more through the Word. But it seemed like every week, as soon as I got to church, something would happen that would cause me to get hurt. Then my hurt would turn into anger (because that was the only emotion I really knew how to express). I would be so upset that I would miss out on any possible positive communication with my friends, worship, and the message. I would just sit in my pew, consumed with the thought of what had just happened. Then, of course, I would think about everything else that had happened in the past to hurt me, especially with the person who had just hurt me again. Every Sunday I would leave church miserable, missing out on anything God was trying to do in me while I was there. One day I realized that I was always unhappy at church. I cried out to God. *"God, I don't like feeling this way,"* I said. *"I don't want to feel like this anymore. Show me what is going on!"*

During my appointment, I explained to my advisor that I felt like I might be compulsive, and I wanted to know why. She asked me for an example. I told her that if I was studying for a test and decided to get a snack to eat, I could not concentrate on studying until I had thrown the papers from the snack in the trash. I had done this many times. I would try as hard as I could to focus on studying, and all I could think about was that paper that needed to be thrown away. I would literally have to get up and throw it away before I could continue with my studies.

My advisor told me that what I was doing was definitely compulsive behavior, and then my advisor took me through a series of questions, as follows.

Advisor: What is the worst thing that would happen if you didn't throw the paper away?

Me: (After long consideration and a little more prompting from her) Someone might see it lying there.

Advisor: And what is the worst thing that would happen if someone came over to your house and saw trash lying around in your house?

Notice the way she worded that, instead of saying, "if someone saw that paper."

Me: They might think I didn't keep my house clean.

Advisor: And what is the worst thing that could happen if someone thought you didn't keep your house clean?

I had to think long and hard about that one, and she had to ask several questions to get me to the true conclusion. My response: "They might think I was worthless."

That was the hardest statement I had ever made in my life. I have always thought myself to be a pretty self-confident person. God has blessed me with several talents, and I do these things well. Because I am outgoing and I have an A-type personality, I never consciously thought that someone might think of me as worthless.

I left that meeting with my advisor a bit depressed. I didn't really know what to do with this information.

I am always so thankful that I have God to turn to in difficult times. I was in another one of those situations where I needed His help. I wanted to know if I really did feel this way about myself, and if I did, why? Then I asked Him to show me how to overcome those feelings. God gave me such a revelation of knowledge that I began to cry. He showed me how the situation at church and the way I was feeling about myself were related. I was constantly getting hurt at church because I was feeling rejected. I would see two of my friends exchanging gifts at Christmas time, and I would feel hurt because I had done everything I could to be good friends with both these people and neither of them had gotten me a gift. I would see people going to lunch together and no one invited me, or doing other activities together where I wasn't included. I was always feeling left out, not important, not liked, and all the other "*nots*" you could say right there. Those feelings were directly related to my feelings of worthlessness. In actuality, we use the term "*worthless*" in counseling, but the real feeling is rejection. Worthless feelings are feelings where we don't feel we are *"valuable enough"* to have love, friendship, attention, etc., just by being ourselves. We feel like we have to be someone we are not to get people to accept us. So when we feel we have fallen short of our own expectations, such as being perfect, we then feel like we are not worth being loved and accepted, (See Chapter 6 of this book on *"Unrealistic Expectations"*) which leads to feelings of rejection, with thoughts such as, *"others don't love and accept people like me"*. So the hurt I was feeling from my perception of rejection and my perfectionism were based in the same thing. I felt that I had to be perfect or someone would reject me. I felt rejected because people didn't include me in their activities. I suddenly realized that I didn't have a true perception of myself.

The next step of this process was very difficult for me. I have always been a very involved person. That, too, goes along with my personality type. I am always busy at something. The Lord spoke very clearly to me that He wanted me to quit doing everything I was doing because my motives were wrong. You see, I was doing the things I was doing so I would feel accepted by the people I was around, instead of doing them out of love for the Lord and for service to Him. Now, all along I thought I was doing these things for the Lord. But He opened my eyes to see my real motives. I enjoyed the praise I received after completing a project that was successful. It was very difficult for me to go to my pastor and tell him I was stepping out of ministry until I got my motives right. I was responsible for several different things in the church, like planning most of the holiday parties/dinners, interior decorating, planting and maintaining flowers outside, and making banners for the sanctuary. To be honest, I was afraid someone would take over doing what I had been responsible for and do a better job. My flesh was screaming loudly! But I knew God had told me to do it, so I didn't have a choice.

After I stepped down from all of my responsibilities and spent time with God through reading His Word and praying, He began to show me how I developed the root of rejection in my life. The misunderstanding of my mental disease (ADD), along with the abuse that I endured, cultivated within me that sense of feeling unwanted, that I would never be good enough, that I was a troublemaker, etc. So, beginning as a child, I learned to cope in unhealthy and destructive ways. As an adult, those coping mechanisms magnified, and I never even knew it. I had been through Christian counseling, and I was in my sixth year of counseling classes before I understood why I was like I was. I prayed for deliverance, and my faithful God did just that. He miraculously healed me from all the rejection issues I had been struggling with and restored to me all the things the enemy had spent years stealing from me. He showed me that I am okay just like I am. I don't have to impress anyone to be liked. People like me just for me. I finally realize that who I am in Christ is what is really important, not who I am to others. I also realize that it is okay if someone doesn't like me. There is such a freedom in being yourself instead of who you think others want you to be.

Now you have read several pages about my life and rejection, and you are probably wondering what all this has to do with anger management. The discovery of my true "*self*" was my first step in anger management. Most of the anger I experienced was due to things in my own life that were messed up, not what other people were doing, like I had always thought. I really believed that people "*made*" me mad and I didn't have a choice in the matter. Having the understanding that I am okay just being me, opened my eyes up to a whole new world about myself, including the fact that I don't have to allow other people to control my emotions.

I used to get angry and discipline my children based on what I thought others would think of me because of their actions (and reject me). Now, I understand that I should discipline my children because I want them to grow into healthy, responsible adults (which was always somewhere in the back of my mind, but not my real motive in discipline). I used to get angry when I didn't get my way or when someone told me that I was wrong about something. Now I understand that the only reason I always had to prove I was right was because if someone thought I was wrong, they might also think I was dumb and then reject me. I now know that I don't have to agree with everyone else and they don't have to agree with me. And, along with that, just because others don't agree with me, it doesn't mean they will reject me. My children or my husband don't have to be perfect because people do not reject me or like me based on how my family acts. If my home isn't perfect when people come over, that's okay. They now know I am normal, instead of perfect (which nobody really believed before anyway, I just hoped they did).

Masks are the different "*faces*" we wear depending on the environment we are in. We put masks on to prevent rejection. We use them to cover up the areas we don't want people to see. We may wear one mask at church, another in front of extended family and friends, and a totally different mask when we are with close family and friends. Usually the mask we wear at home is not even close to being the same as the ones we wear in public. Yes, we even wear masks around those closest to us, because there are things deep down within us that we don't even want them to know about.

The problem with wearing masks is the pressure that results from trying to keep them on. If the wrong one comes off in the wrong circumstance, people might see the real us that we didn't want them to know about. Many angry people only express their anger around those they are really close to. Around everyone else, they keep that mask tight and secure. Sometimes, however, unexpected things happen, and the anger comes out from under the mask, and it does so in front of people who didn't know it was there. We are embarrassed, and they are in shock. Having an understanding of who we really are, beneath all the masks, relieves a lot of internal pressure. The more we learn about ourselves and who we are in Christ, the more of the mask we can take off remove.

Reading and studying God's Word, and allowing it to penetrate our very nature, will help us to lay those masks down. As we memorize and quote scriptures about who God says we are, we begin to believe them instead of the negative things we have thought about ourselves for most of our lives. As God helps us to change the way we feel about ourselves, He also heals the past hurts and disappointments, and He delivers us from the fear of rejections. Jesus experienced rejection so we wouldn't have to (Isaiah 53:3, Mark 9:12, Luke 9:22, Luke 17:25).[1] The work has already been done. It was completed in the death and resurrection of our Lord Jesus Christ. We only have to believe and receive it. We do that by applying the Word of God to our lives.

CHAPTER 6
Unrealistic Expectations

Unrealistic expectations are assumptions that we place on other people, or ourselves, and are based on our past, our knowledge, and our experiences. They are unreasonable and can cause a lot of anger and hurt. Sometimes we place unrealistic expectations on others around us because we have so many on ourselves.

I became a perfectionist at a young age; therefore, I expected my husband and children to also be perfect, or at least strive for perfection. I was constantly angry because they fell short of my expectations. Both my sons are very intelligent, and they have the ability to be very successful. When they were in elementary school, they made straight A's on all their report cards. Because they were capable of A's, I expected only A's. When my older son started junior high, he became more interested in sports than he did his grades. He still made mostly A's, but he would bring home an occasional B, and I would be furious. My younger son did well through junior high, but in high school he began to care more about music, skateboards, and girls than his grades. Again, I would become furious over anything less than an A. Now, I'm not talking about getting a little disappointed, I'm talking about rage. I would scream and yell and rant and rave; I would ground them "*forever*" from everything. I was ridiculous, but I didn't know it then. I expected my children to be perfect, and nothing less than that was acceptable. I had very unrealistic expectations of them.

I was the same outrageous person to my husband. I would expect my house to be spotless when I came home. If it wasn't, everyone would experience my wrath, especially my husband. I would gripe at him because he didn't hang clothes the way I wanted them, clean the way I did, or discipline the children the way I thought he should. I griped about everything he did. It is a wonder he didn't leave me years ago. I was discussing this dilemma with my mother one day, and she said something astonishing to me. She said I was expecting too much of him.

Growing up, I was taught how to clean, do laundry, and all those household chores that only girls were taught when I was young. My husband was not taught those skills before we got married. He was raised in a home with five males and one female. His mother did all the housework. So for me to expect that my husband would know how to clean like I did was unrealistic. My mom told me to be happy that he was doing something and accept what he did do instead of complaining about what he didn't do. I couldn't believe my mother took his side. I learned not to call her when I was angry with my husband. That was very hard for me to swallow, so I didn't. Years later when I thought back on this, I realized how right my mom was.

Let me tell you a funny story about Brad and I. One night I was making pizza for dinner, and I asked him to run to the store and get pizza cheese. Now, I first need to explain that Brad is one of the most intelligent people I have ever met—literally. But he has absolutely no common sense. I, on the other hand, am not the most intelligent person; I have to work very hard at things like grades. But I have a lot of common sense. It took me years to realize that this was one of our biggest differences and biggest fight instigators. So back to the story—Brad came home with Parmesan cheese. Now I know some of you, mostly males, reading this are saying to yourself, "*So?*" And others, mostly females, are probably saying, "*Typical!*" The truth is, Brad sprinkles Parmesan cheese on his pizza, so to him that was pizza cheese. Those of us who have made pizza before know that you can't "*make*" pizza with Parmesan cheese; you need mozzarella cheese. Funny as this may seem, this was the type of thing Brad and I constantly fought about for years. I would ask him to do something that I thought very simple, but he never really understood what I was expecting, especially when it came to running to the grocery store. Several years ago, I came to a startling conclusion. Either I had to stop what I was doing to run to the store myself when I needed something, or accept what Brad brought home, no matter what it was or how ridiculous it was. I am much more specific now. I make detailed lists. I sometimes take a photo of the item with my cell phone and text it to him so he can actually see a picture of what I am wanting.

My expectations are based on my life experiences, and I cannot expect anyone else to say, feel, or think the same way I do, because they have their own life experiences. When we have unrealistic expectations on ourselves, we set ourselves up for failure. I have known many people who have set unrealistic goals for themselves after high school. Then, when, by a certain age, they had not reached their goals, it devastated them. My own observation is that this happens to many men when they reach about forty years old and women when they reach thirty. Reality of where they are and what they have or haven't accomplished hits them.

I remember two specific instances where this has happened.

This man I know, let's call him Steve, reached forty and realized he hadn't accomplished enough in his life so he decided he was going to be a country western singer. He started frequenting bars where they had karaoke so that he could sing along with prerecorded music and do it in public. He visited them more and more often until he was in the bars almost every night. He met a woman who owned one of the karaoke set-ups, who traveled different nights to different bars, and he began following her from bar to bar. Soon they were dating. Now, at the same time that was going on he had a wife and three children, two of which were teenagers, the other about eleven years old. It wasn't long before he asked his wife for a divorce. This devastated his whole family. See, Steve couldn't accept where he was in life because he had not accomplished what he thought he *"should have"* by the age of forty. He felt like a failure because he had set goals for himself that he hadn't reached. These were unrealistic expectations of himself. His sense of failure ended up ruining his marriage.

The other instance is a friend of mine I will call Tory. She is several years younger than I am. She has been married for about seven years, and she and her husband have done pretty well financially. They both have professional jobs, and they have two young boys. The problem is that Tory turned thirty last year, and she began to evaluate where she was in life and found she wasn't happy. Her thirtieth birthday was so difficult for her that she wouldn't allow us to give her a birthday party, and no one could talk to her about it.

Now, almost a year later, she is trying to figure out what to do to make the changes needed to get herself where she thinks she belongs. Tory has a tendency to compare her life to mine and be disappointed that she hasn't accomplished the same things Brad and I have. She has a hard time seeing the reality that Brad and I have been married more than forty two years, and there have been a lot of struggles through those years. It is very unrealistic for her to set goals for herself to be where we are after forty two years, when she has only been married seven. She doesn't see the truth: that she has accomplished much more in her seven years than we did in that same amount of time. She and her husband are doing very well, but there are always struggles with young adults, young marriages, and young children. Our children have their own lives now. We don't have to deal with the aspect of having children at home any longer. Tory, by comparing herself to me, has set unrealistic expectations of her life, instead of looking at who she is and that what she has accomplished is good. The unrealistic expectations have led Tory to become unnecessarily angry with both herself and her circumstances.

The other way unrealistic expectations can be unhealthy is when we place them on others. I was in the process of learning about them myself when I had a perfect example happen in my own life. On the first birthday of my oldest grandson Levi, he fell and busted his eyebrow open while he and his mom were at our home. Our home became instant chaos. My daughter-in-law, Blake, freaked out when she saw the blood. Head injuries tend to bleed more, so there was quite a bit of blood.

My husband scooped him up, and I got a rag to put on it. Poor Blake was a mess. She was crying as much as the baby was. Because my husband and I never want to try to take over or make our kids think we are trying to take their place, we kept asking her if she wanted him and if it was okay that we were doing what we were to take care of him. She was so distraught she didn't care what we were doing as long as we were taking care of him. In the back of my mind, I was thinking that she needed to quit freaking out and take care of her son.

Now, my and my husband's reactions to accidents are based on our past experiences. Our oldest son and Blake's husband, Bradley, was an accident-prone kid. Every time we turned around, we were taking him to the hospital for something. He had a lot of weird and extreme accidents when he was growing up. Brad and I had to learn how to not freak out when he got hurt but to calmly take care of the situation. So a little cut on the head was no big deal to us, nor was it to our son. Of course Blake called him as soon as the accident happened, and he came home. When he walked in and saw Levi's head, he just shrugged his shoulders and said, *"Oh, that's nothing."* Now, remember, this kid has been to the emergency room more times than we could count. He might have thought it was a big deal if Levi's arm was cut off or something major, but to him, this was nothing. Blake was furious at him. She couldn't believe he was not making a big deal out of it.

Can you see the process of unrealistic expectations unraveling here? First, I thought Blake should act differently. She did not grow up going to the emergency room all the time. This was her first child and his first accident. I was totally wrong to expect to her to act any way other than the way she did; Blake acted very realistically for her and her experiences. Then Blake got upset because Bradley didn't react in the same way she did. But for him, in comparison to what he has been through, Levi was fine. Blake had unrealistic expectations on Bradley to feel about her son the same way she did.

I did not see the humor in this situation until later when I was thinking about it in relation to unrealistic expectations. It was a real eye opener for me, and a great example to use when teaching anger management.

Although this is a simple illustration, it shows how quickly we can get angry when we expect others to act or feel the same way we do.

There are a lot of other ways I have had unrealistic expectations of other people. When I worked in retail as a manager, I had a difficult time working with slow people. I do everything fast, and I get very irritated when I am working with someone who doesn't catch on easily or as quickly as I do. I would just send them to do something on their own and finish the job at hand by myself. Not the greatest management skills, huh? I would also get irritated when I was checking out at a store and the clerk was slow. It was difficult for me to stand still and not say something rude. I wanted to tell her to move out of the way and let me do it myself. I can even get aggravated if the person driving in front of me doesn't take off as fast as I want them to. I always want to be the first person at the stoplight so I can take off without waiting for anyone else. These are all examples of how I have personally placed my own unrealistic expectations on other people. I could list probably a hundred more ways I do this type of thing. I have had to learn to talk myself through these situations so that I am not a nervous wreck all the time like I used to be.

Unrealistic expectations are based on shoulds and needs within our own minds: "*He should act a certain way,*" "she *shouldn't talk like that,*" "*they or you need to...*" "*I should be doing something different.*" One of the exercises I do when I teach anger management is to have the clients write out all the shoulds and needs they have in their own lives. They will each list on a piece of paper all the things they can think about that they do but feel they shouldn't and list all the things they think they need to be doing but aren't. Then we take time to discuss their lists. I ask them questions like, "*Why do you think you should be doing that?*" Most of the time, their answers are based on expectations of themselves or others that are very unrealistic for their *"real life situations."*

I did this with a girl friend of mine who was struggling with her life. She has four children—ages seven, five, three, and one. She and her husband run a business, and they live hundreds of miles from all their family and close friends. Plus, she and her husband have both struggled with some major health issues. She was beating herself up one day because she couldn't get up early in the morning and read her Bible for hours every day. As I discussed with her the reasons she thought she should do this, it became evident that she had placed a law on herself about reading the Bible that was based on what she had heard all the great teachers and preachers say.

Each of us is in a different situation in our lives. It wasn't until both my boys were in elementary school before I could realistically spend hours in the Word, praying, and spending time with God. I helped her to realize that her ministry right now was her family. That is where God had her at this time in her life. Don't get me wrong here. I think it is very important that we each spend quality time with God every day. But what is quality to some is not necessarily quality to others. I helped my friend decide on a realistic amount of time to set aside to spend with God. We discussed the best time of day for her to do this and what she could reasonably plan for herself. It is always better to begin with small, realistic goals and build up instead of setting big goals that are impossible to accomplish, causing you to feel like a failure when you give up. This is discussed further in Chapter 11—Goal Setting. My friend felt a huge release of internal pressure when she realized that she didn't have to live up to others' expectations of her or even the expectations she had set for herself.

A man named Tony had a bad day at work. His computer crashed, and he lost all the work he had done that week. He left the job that afternoon feeling very discouraged. As he approached the door that exited his building, he realized it had begun to rain. He didn't have his umbrella. By the time he got to his car, he was soaked. As he turned the key to start his car, he found the battery was dead. Could things get any worse? We have all had these kinds of days— days where we want to crawl back in bed and start over. Typically, we get more and more discouraged as the day goes on, because it feels like things keep getting worse. Then, if we have unrealistic expectations on others, or ourselves, and they fall through, we set ourselves up for an explosion. Let's see what happened to Tony.

When he finally got his car started and headed for home, be began to think about his wife and children. He visualized his wife at home cooking dinner and his children in their rooms working quietly on their homework. He talked to himself, *"At least I can go to my nice, clean home, take a warm shower, eat a hot home-cooked meal, and relax on the couch in front of the TV for the rest of the night."* The truth was, Tony's wife also worked. She rushed from her job, picked the kids up from daycare, stopped at the store to pick up some necessities, and rushed home to quickly throw something together for dinner, while she fought with the kids about their homework. Tony's kids were typical kids who had not been home with their parents or each other all day. They started fighting the minute they got in the car, and it only got worse as they arrived home. Tony came home to an exhausted wife, a dinner of cold hot dogs and chips, screaming and crying kids, and a couch covered in laundry that hadn't been folded and put away. Tony blew. He yelled at his wife and his kids, then stomped to his room, slammed the door, and fell into the bed, ready to burst into tears.

Instead of self-talking realistically, Tony self-talked unrealistically, trying to make himself feel better about his crummy day. If Tony would have prepared himself for what his home was typically like when he got home from work, then made plans for what he was going to do when he got there, he could have avoided the explosion. Tony could have planned to ignore everything he saw when he walked in the door, said hi to his wife and kids, and then went straight to his room to shower and relax before encountering the tasks of father and husband.

Tony and his wife could have discussed making these changes where they both could have some quiet time before tackling their responsibilities at home. They could set rules with the kids about what they were to do for the first thirty minutes after arriving home—maybe spend that time in their rooms alone, so their parents could also have some alone time. Maybe mom could relax in the tub with soft music and dimmed lights or read a chapter of a book before dealing with cooking and homework. Maybe dad could shower and read the newspaper or watch the news in his room by himself before approaching the family. They might need to switch off every other day with quiet times after work, depending on the age and responsibility level of their children.

Looking at life realistically is very freeing. Expecting things to be different than they are is failure waiting to happen. We watch TV, movies, read books, etc., of the way perfect families are *"supposed"* to be, then we want ours to be the same way. But those situations are not real. They are money-making, fictionalized stories created for the purpose of getting attention. Writers, producers, etc., know what the public wants, so they produce it. We watch it more and more, and then we want it more and more. Whether it is wanting perfect families, perfect bodies, perfect sex, or perfect things—like homes and cars—it is unrealistic.

There was only one perfect man. His name was Jesus. There will never be another. We can strive to be more like him, and with his help we can come closer to that goal. But expecting perfection is impossible. In doing so, we set ourselves up for failure. Again, I am not talking about setting goals and working realistically toward those goals. That is totally different than unrealistic expectations. Setting realistic goals is healthy. Unrealistic expectations are unhealthy and can cause great pain and discouragement.

Take some time to look at the shoulds and needs you have about yourself and others. Write them out on paper. Talk to someone you are close to, someone you trust. Ask them to help you see if they are realistic or unrealistic. If they are realistic, keep them. If they aren't, throw them out and make new ones, ones that are realistic for you and your life. This is one of the most freeing things I have ever done in my life. It is not easy, because it has taken years of us thinking this way to come to where we are today. But, hard as it is, it is not impossible, and it is well worth the work invested into changing the way we think.

CHAPTER 7
We Want Our Way

One night when I was teaching an anger management class to our youth group, I asked them, "*What do you get angry about?*" Kids have such wonderful insight, and for the most part, they are brutally honest. A couple of the girls admitted that most of their anger was because they didn't get their way. Wow! As I thought about that for a while, I realized that this statement is true for everyone. We get angry as a result of not getting our way. It does not matter what the cause of the anger is, whether injustice, frustrations, irritations, or abuse, the bottom line is that we want things a certain way and we get angry when it doesn't happen. James 4:1–2a says, "*What causes fights and quarrels among you? Don't they come from your desires that battle within you? You want something but don't get it.*"

Let's take, for example, that our kids are being disobedient and we have said something to them about it for the millionth time. I remember this well from when my boys were young. I would repeat the same thing over and over to them until I was practically blue in the face, but they continued to disobey. I would end up getting angry then yelling and screaming at them. Then I would do something unrealistic like ground them to their room for a month, which was not very practical and something I would never follow through with. What was the real reason I was angry? I wanted them to obey me, and they would not. I wanted my way and didn't get it. Here's another example: Someone owes you money, and they are not paying it back as agreed. You get angry with them. Then they begin to avoid you because they know they owe you money and aren't paying you, which causes you even more anger.

I also saw this same type of behavior from my four grandsons when they were toddlers. The two oldest grandsons Levi and Hayden, at three years old, would throw a huge crying temper fit when they wanted to stay with Grandma and Grandpa and were not allowed to. Ethan, at age two, said "*no*" over and over and began to hit his head when he didn't get his way. Noah, who was also two, would sit on the floor and cry, with a really sad face, when things didn't go the way he wanted them to. I could give thousands more of these types of examples, and they would all boil down to the same basic principle: we get angry when we don't get our way.

This may seem like a simple thing to realize, and you may be wondering how knowing this can help you to overcome your anger problem, but the truth is it can do exactly that. The next time you find yourself angry about something, take a second and try to realize what it is about this situation that is really causing the anger. Try to figure out what you are wanting and not getting. Do you feel you are being treated unjustly? Do you feel like someone is trying to take advantage of you? Do you feel disrespected? Do you feel like you are being abused? What is the triggering force behind the anger? Knowing the source is another step to recognizing and eventually overcoming anger.

Nobody likes to feel taken advantage of, disrespected, abused, or mistreated in any way. Many times the anger that results from these things is justified. But, if you can recognize why you are feeling the way you are, you can stop the feeling from getting out of hand. Using the example above about the children being disobedient, I can say to myself, *"What is it about this situation that is triggering the anger to rise in me?"* The truth is, I want my kids to respect me by minding, and they are not. As I realize that I am upset because I am not getting my way, I can talk myself through the situation without losing my temper. At this point you begin to use the techniques taught in Chapter 2 of this book, titled *"Self-Talk."*

Sometimes wanting our way is part of wanting to be noticed or not wanting to feel left out. I saw this happen over and over as I worked with the youth in our previous church, mostly with the girls. There were times where this has happened and it was so obvious that everyone in the youth group noticed it except the person doing it.

Let me give you an example. Most of the youth in our group had grown up together; therefore, they spent a lot of time together. When any two of the girls would begin to spend more time with each other than the rest of the group, anger would arise. The reasons these two specific girls were spending more time together could be very logical—a parent out of town or one helping the other with homework. When this would happen, there would be at least one girl who would begin to feel left out. Instead of talking to the other two girls about what she was feeling, she would allow the anger to build, basing it on the thoughts the enemy was putting in her head.

He would say things like, *"They are talking about you!"* or *"They are mad at you!"* or *"They just don't like you anymore!"* This girl would try to think of anything she had done to cause them to be angry with her or to hurt their feelings, and she might even develop some idiotic explanation to herself as to why they were "*leaving her out.*" But even that did not reduce the feelings of anger she was experiencing from feeling left out.

This feeling of anger, by the way, is really rooted in hurt, and it is a result of feeling rejected. This teenager, who was feeling left out, was angry because she was not getting her way. She wanted to be noticed, she wanted to be part of the "*group*," and she didn't feel like she was. She then, in turn, would start acting ugly toward them. She would do this in several different ways. She would snap at them when they tried to talk to her. She would purposely ask an "*outsider*" to spend the night at her house, making sure the others knew. And she would totally ignore them. Then the whole process would begin again, but from the other direction, the other two girls trying to figure out what she was upset about.

I would observe this process for several days, maybe even a week or so, to see if they worked it out between themselves, but many times I would need to call them all together for a talk. When I would get them actually talking to each other about what was going on and explaining their feelings to each other, they would realize there wasn't really a problem at all.

I will give you another example which will really hit home with many of you reading this book—speeding. Why is it that we get so angry about the way other people drive? My husband, Brad, gets very angry when we are going the speed limit and someone flies around us. He will honk the horn and flash his headlights at the person, like that is really going to make any difference in the way this person is driving. Brad wants to make sure that the other person knows he doesn't like what they are doing.

Now don't get me wrong here. I am not saying that people who drive crazy are right. My point is, Brad doesn't like other people driving like that because he would like to do the same thing himself, but because of maturity, safety, and the conviction of the Holy Spirit (and his wife) he can no longer drive that way. In reality, other people speeding, whether they are going five or fifty miles per hour over the speed limit, should have no effect on us at all. It is their money (for possible speeding tickets) that is at risk. But, because we think it is not right and we can't control it and we aren't getting our way, we get angry.

It is really amazing how we allow so many things in life to control how we feel. It is even more amazing how ridiculous many of those things that we get angry about are. The Bible tells us in 1 Peter 5:8 to *"Be sober, be vigilant; because your adversary the devil walks about like a roaring lion, seeking whom he may devour"* (KJV, emphasis added). Notice the word I italicized in that scripture—the word *"may."* Webster's Dictionary[1] defines the word may as *"having permission to"* do something. The enemy can only do as much in our lives as we allow him or give him permission to do. Many times he puts thoughts in our heads, and we believe them. Then we take ownership of those thoughts, as if they were the truth. Then we allow other thoughts to build on the first one, and then another and another, until those thoughts consume us, and we become angry. Many times the first thought will bring anger up inside of us. That is why it is so important to recognize that first thought, then self-talk ourselves through the situation before it gets out of hand.

In the example I gave earlier about my youth group, the situation could have been avoided if the girl feeling left out would not have believed the lies the enemy was putting in her head. Had she known to self-talk, she could have rationalized that approaching them about her feelings was the best thing to do. Her self-talk could include the following: *"Hmm...I wonder why they are spending so much time together? Is it possible they are leaving me out for a reason? I should just talk to them and find out. That will help me to not get upset about something that might not even be true."* Then, she could casually walk up to them and ask them, *"What's up? Your dad out of town again?"* or something to that effect. By doing this, she would have stopped the enemy in his tracks. She would not become the *"may"* 1 Peter 5:8 is talking about.

This is an ongoing process that should last a lifetime. We all have different moments in our lives where we become more defensive than others. There are instances when getting our way is more important than not. There are also seasons when we are struggling with several different things at once. If our stress level is high, if we aren't feeling physically well, if we have had emotional strains (like the death of a loved one), we can tend to be more sensitive to other's words and actions than normal. As we begin to learn this process of recognizing why we are angry and learning how to overcome the anger, we can also learn to recognize those more tense times in our lives. From there we can mentally make decisions about the correct ways to respond, based on our levels of tenseness and our past reactions. The answer may be to go away, to relax by ourselves, to take time-outs, to call a babysitter, etc. The most important factor is recognition. After learning how to recognize that we are angry because we are not getting our way, it is usually pretty easy to stop the anger from getting out of hand. Then, in many instances, we can laugh at ourselves for getting angry about ridiculous things.

Parents can begin to instill in their children this process of working through thoughts when they are old enough to communicate. Depending on their maturity level, a three- or four-year-old may be developed enough to understand this process. When children show anger because they are not getting their way, parents can begin to discuss the child's feelings with them. They can help the child try to identify the cause of the feeling. The cause may be simple: they are angry because they aren't getting their way. But helping children recognize their own feelings and identifying the cause of those feelings is helping them develop anger management skills they will use the rest of their lives.

This can be difficult for the parent. When a child gets angry because he is not getting his way, many times the parent will in turn get angry with the child. It is even more difficult if the parent is also struggling with anger in his or her own life. It is never too late to begin working with children in this way. I did this with the teenagers in my youth group all the time. When they were angry about something, I would allow them to talk about it for a while, and then I would begin asking them questions, which would cause them to have to think about what is really going on.

There is a very important element to remember when trying to help a person work through anger issues: there must be a good, existing relationship between the two people, the one with the problem and the one trying to help (a parent/child relationship for example). Otherwise, the situation could be potentially dangerous because trying to help can end up hurting instead. Many people view help as criticism, especially if they have a defensive or rebellious type personality.

CHAPTER 8
Act or React

When we feel like we are losing control of a situation or have already lost control, we tend to experience anger. What we do from that point on is based on the choices we make. Do we calmly act in a difficult situation, or do we react and make the situation worse? Let's look at what Webster's[1] says about acting and reacting. Pay particular attention to the contrast of the two words:

Act - accomplishment, action, deed, do or doing, operation, perform

React - respond to stimulus, resistance, action in opposite direction to another, backlash, counteraction

There is a huge difference between acting and reacting. Acting is an accomplishment. If we can learn to act, to think consciously about what we are doing when we feel ourselves becoming angry, we can learn to overcome the reaction, which is a learned response. Here are a couple of other words for you to consider:

Impulsive - motion produced by a sudden applied force, push, incitement, influence, instigate, sudden thought

Cautious - careful, prudent, discreet, level headed, guarded, calculated, reserved, safe, conscientious, discerning

When we react, we are being impulsive. When we act, we are being cautious. Think of an actor. He spends a long time memorizing his part. He studies and repeats it until it becomes a part of him. Then he knows what the next step or word is when the time is right. We can do the same thing. We can learn the right way to act in any given situation. We can teach ourselves to think through the situation before responding. We can prevent ourselves from reacting by acting. We must think first then act in response to difficult stimulus, instead of reacting impulsively. To learn how to think things through before reacting see Chapter 2 of this book, titled "*Self-Talk.*"

This is another area where memorizing scripture can help us. Quoting scriptures like "*No weapon formed against me will prosper* [2]*,*" "*Greater is he that is in me than he that is in the world* [3]*,*" and "*I submit to the Lord and I rebuke the enemy, and he must flee* [4]" will help you to quickly become focused and realize that you do not want the enemy (or the flesh) to win in your difficult situation.

One of the main things to remember about anger is that it usually comes up inside us quickly, so you have to learn how to recognize and stop it quickly. One of the most important things to do is to recognize the first "*feelings*" of anger arising. Ask yourself, "*What changes does my body go through when I get angry?*" Some examples of body changes are: sweaty palms, upset stomach, headache or head throbbing, shaking, rapid heartbeat, knees knocking, gripping fists. There are many other ways your body can tell you that anger is rising. The next time you feel angry, stop and think about what is going on in your body. Once you can begin to recognize that first bodily response, it will help you to recognize that you are getting angry and then you can learn to act in response instead of reacting.

Sometimes we have to work through or plan what we will do in order to act appropriately when we feel anger arise in us. Memorizing scripture and learning how to self-talk will help that process. We can apply that old saying, "*practice makes perfect,*" when we are talking about relearning how to act when we get angry or to prevent us from getting angry. We have had a lot of practice displaying anger the way we have in the past. Now we must practice thinking and acting instead of reacting.

I will give you a good example. My husband drinks coffee, and a lot of it. It seems like every time he makes a cup, he leaves a mess on the counter. When I go in the kitchen to do something, I see the mess, and my first instinct is to react and yell and scream at him. One day, I did just that. I yelled at him to come into the kitchen, and when he got there, I let him have it. I told him how I was sick and tired of cleaning up his coffee messes and he needed to start cleaning up after himself. He just stood there looking at me, not saying a word. When I was all finished with my temper tantrum, he calmly said, "*I didn't do that. I wasn't even in here.*" Come to find out, my son had run through the kitchen and in the process had hit my husband's coffee cup and spilled the coffee on the counter.

Of course, I wanted to crawl in a hole and hide. I needed to learn to think before reacting. I needed to find out all the information before I exploded. I have now learned how to make myself act in these type situations, instead of reacting. I calm myself, I ask questions, or I just clean up the mess without saying anything.

I think the best part of learning to act instead of react is that it feels good. I used to think that I had to yell and scream to get my opinion heard. I used to think things wouldn't seem as important if I didn't scream about them. I used to think that screaming was the only way of getting a situation under control. And I had to have control, no matter what. Later, after my fits, I would beat myself up for reacting like I did. I felt guilty and foolish for losing it. But I had too much pride to apologize for what I had done. I thought, *I was right in what I had said. I was justified in saying it like I did. Really, the only thing I did wrong was lose my temper. That really wasn't such a bad thing, since I was justified, right?*

Now I realize that I feel so much better when I am in control of myself in a challenging situation, instead of out of control. I sometimes pat myself on the back when I realize how I now act in situations, whereas before I would have reacted in an unacceptable and/or inappropriate way. It feels really good to think through difficult circumstances instead of reacting and making myself feel foolish and guilty.

Feeling guilty isn't from God. Scripture tells us that there is no condemnation in Christ [5]. Scripture also tells us that the Holy Spirit will convict us when we are doing something wrong[6]. Guilt just brings about bad feelings, over and over. It will haunt us if we allow it. Conviction, through the Holy Spirit, shows us that there is a need to change, not to feel guilty. When the Holy Spirit convicts us in an area, He prompts us to repent or turn away from that sin. The enemy will just keep telling us how bad we are, making us feel guilty, but not allowing us forgiveness from God or ourselves.

As we learn to act in place of reacting, we feel good about ourselves, and others like us better. I don't know of very many people who enjoy being around individuals who are always reacting by yelling, screaming, or acting out in other inappropriate ways. The Bible also tells us, *"Out of the overflow of the heart the mouth speaks"*

(Matthew 12:44). Whatever is down inside our heart is going to come out, especially when difficult situations occur. If there is a lot of anger inside, a lot of anger will come out. The more we train ourselves how to act, the more the acting part will become natural and therefore will be in our hearts and will come natural in difficult situations.

Another important thing to remember here is that sometimes the anger we have in our hearts is very deeply rooted. There are people who act out in anger because that is how they were taught by their parents or guardians. There are also those people who have had something happen early in their childhood to cause them to turn to anger as a coping skill. This could have been caused by a variety of different things, including the death of a loved one, abuse of any kind, teasing, a disability, a permanent injury, injustice, etc. If you are one of those people who were deeply hurt in your past and that is the root of your anger, I would like to suggest you seek out professional help in the form of counseling to help you overcome the hurt. A person can learn all the anger management skills available, but if a deep-rooted hurt exists, the anger management skills won't be as effective, and they won't take the hurt away. Counseling, coupled with anger management skills, is really the best overall way to overcome any anger problems, but especially those caused by a history of deeply rooted hurts.

CHAPTER 9
Are You Passive, Aggressive, or Assertive?

Passive people are those who act as if everything is okay all the time. They never stand up for themselves and are therefore constantly being taken advantage of. Passive people are afraid to be honest. If someone asks them if something is wrong, they will always say no. They don't want to rock the boat; they want to be the peacemakers. The problem with being too passive is that on the outside these people seem to be okay, but on the inside they are exploding. Every time someone takes advantage of them, they get angry with themselves for not standing up for themselves. They beat themselves up for not being honest when asked questions. Eventually, the passive person will explode, and when they do, look out.

My husband has spent most of his life being passive. He has always let others have their way so as not to cause problems. He would never take food back at a restaurant and died with humiliation when I did. If someone told him to do something, he did it, no questions asked, even when he thought it to be unfair. There have only been a few times in our marriage that I have seen Brad really angry. He was always the peacemaker between our two boys and me. He was calm and easygoing and wanted everything around him to be that way too. He probably only spanked our children a handful of times their whole lives, but the boys knew they better mind their dad and respect him. Why? Because when he blew, when he really got angry, we all felt the blow. He would yell to the top of his lungs, his eyes would turn red, and he would seem ten feet tall. We all stopped and listened when he got angry. This was because Brad was a stuffer, as most passive people are. He didn't handle situations when confronted with them. He would stuff until he couldn't stuff any longer; then he would blow.

Passive people can only handle the internal pressure for so long. They are like volcanoes. The pressure and heat inside builds for a long time. Then when it is time for them to erupt, the hot, yucky stuff pours out over everything, usually damaging the surrounding environment.

Another problem passive people deal with is that after so many years of being taken advantage of and putting up with other people's stuff, they take an opposite turn. They become aggressive. All the anger that has built up inside of them their whole lives begins to come out all at once for everything they have ever been angry about but kept in.

Aggressive people are just plain mad. They are mad at everyone, for everything, all the time. That was me. It didn't matter what, who, when, where, or why; I would get angry. I probably could not have told you why I was angry at any given time or even admit that I was, but looking back, it is evident that I was. Aggressive people always want their way; they want to win every argument, they always want to be right, they want to satisfy their own needs, and they will do whatever it takes to make sure things go their way. Aggressive people usually don't care if they hurt others. They will actually hurt others to make them feel better about themselves.

Aggressive people are on a power trip. They want power and take it at any cost. They are very controlling people. They want to control every situation they are involved in and every person they are around. Aggressive people feel threatened by others who they perceive as better than them in some way, but they would never allow that person to know they think them better. Actually, they will do just the opposite by trying to put others down. This way, they think they look better to others. Aggressive people usually act tough, wanting others to think they are tough. Appearance is very important to people who are aggressive, so they do whatever they can to look good. They tend to blow up at everything. They are the real yellers and screamers. Many physical abusers are aggressive people. Abusing others gives them power over those people. Other aggressive people choose to hit things like walls, cars, furniture, or they throw things, thinking this will help them prove their point better. Aggressive people love it when others are scared of them.

On the outside, aggressive people look like they have it all together. Many passive people look at aggressive people and wish they were more like them. Reality is that the aggressive person is just as unhappy inside as the passive person. They carry around a lot of guilt about the people and things they have hurt, but they have no idea how to change how they are.

Assertiveness is the happy medium. Assertive people work with facts and do so in a calm, cool, collected manner, but they get their point across. They don't have to yell or scream; they don't have to hit or scare. They state the facts in an authoritative manner, and they usually get what they want by doing so. Assertive people do not need to control others, nor do they allow others to control them. They stand up for themselves, but they do it in an appropriate way. Assertive people know how to say no to others without feeling guilty for doing so. They are concerned about what is in their best interest, but not to the extent of taking advantage of or hurting others. Assertive people are usually happy with themselves. They respect others, they can express their true feelings when asked, and they can acknowledge their own mistakes and faults without being concerned that others will see them in a negative light.

Let's look at how differently the passive, aggressive, and assertive people would handle the same situation. Here's an example: A bill comes in the mail that has already been paid.

Passive people would pay the bill again, angry with themselves because they didn't have the nerve to call the company and set things straight.

Aggressive people would react by calling the company and yelling at whoever answered the phone. They would not take the time to think through the situation but would immediately respond in a negative way, then feel guilty later for doing so.

Assertive people would take the time to look at the facts of the situation instead of immediately responding. They would get out the checkbook and find what check number they used to pay the bill. They would then call the company and ask for the appropriate person to talk to about it. They would explain to this person that they received a bill they had already paid. They would give the person on the phone the date, check number, and amount of the check they wrote and then tell the person they would be happy to send a copy of the check, if needed, to clear up the account. Now, which of these three people do you think got the best results?

There are several ways the passive person and the aggressive person can work toward becoming more assertive. First of all, think! As with all control over anger, you must take the time to think—to act instead of react. It may help for you to take out a piece of paper and write out what you think a correct response might be. This can help you with your self-talk. Practice what you might say to another person until you are comfortable saying it. Maybe even talk to someone you trust who can help you develop the best possible response. Start with little things—for example, the bill we just discussed. Before paying the bill, or making the phone call, write out what you think would be appropriate to say when you do call. Call a friend and read to them what you have written out. Ask them to be honest and help you develop a good response. Then make the phone call. After you have done this a few times, you will realize how good it feels and you will want to do it this way more often. Your old way of responding is habit. You have to break that habit.

Always try to stay in the positive when you talk to others. Use *"I"* statements instead of *"you"* statements. Whenever you approach people with a *"you"* statement, they almost always get on the defense. Instead of saying, *"You sent me a bill I have already paid,"* say, *"I received a bill in the mail today which I have already paid."* Instead of saying, *"You made me angry when you did that,"* say, *"I felt angry when that happened."* Instead of saying, *"Why did you say that to me?"* say, *"I felt hurt when you said that."* Simply changing your *"you's"* to *"I's"* can make a big difference in your communication skills. Assertiveness is about communication. It is about getting your point across, which is important, without hurting others or without others hurting you.

Say no when you need to say no. Try it. When others ask you to do something and you really don't want to do it, say no. If they are really your friend, if they really love you, they will accept your answer, whatever it may be. People who get angry with you because you tell them no are usually the very people who take advantage of you. These types of people are users. They want everyone to do things for them and usually don't do anything for others. Many people who get mad when told no are aggressive people. That is why they don't like being told no. They want their way. After you have said no a few times, you will build confidence in yourself. Only do for others the things you want to do, not the things you are afraid to say no to. The only way to overcome this type of fear is to do it afraid. After you have done it afraid a few times, you won't be afraid any longer.

When you are angry about something, state your anger and why. It is okay to feel anger, and it is okay to tell others you are angry, but it is important to do so in a proper way. If you feel someone is taking advantage of you, tell him or her so. Say, "*I feel like you are trying to take advantage of me in this situation.*" You don't have to stuff the feeling, and you don't have to yell or scream either. Just state the fact. Don't allow others to intimidate you. If you don't feel right about something, say so. If they don't like it, it is their problem, not yours. You have a right to state what you think and feel, as long as you do so in appropriate ways where you are standing up for your rights, without taking advantage of others.

CHAPTER 10
Seeing Others' Perspectives

I once heard a story about a woman who got on a public bus with her three children. She went to the back and sat down by herself. Her children went wild. They were climbing all over the other passengers, getting into their personal belongings, making loud noises, and basically irritating the other people on the bus. The mother, oblivious to what her children were doing, was sitting quietly, staring out the window of the bus. One of the male passengers finally had enough of the children, and he approached the mother. *"Ma'am, I am very sorry to bother you, but your children are being very disruptive. Can you please do something to settle them down?"*

Now before I finish this story, I want you to think for a moment about what you would do in this same situation. I know if I were in a bus with a bunch of wild kids, my natural reaction would be to get angry and say something rude to the mom or to the children. Let's see what happened next.

The mother apologized to the man and then made the following statement: *"I just left the hospital. My children's father has just passed away, and I am trying to figure out what we are going to do now."*

Did your viewpoint suddenly change? This story model is called a *"paradigm shift."* When you are going one direction and something happens to make you totally change the way you were going, that is called a paradigm shift. In this story, you are irritated at this mother for not caring for her children. After hearing her explanation, did you change your attitude? Did you suddenly want to find a way to help her instead of being angry with her?

This type of situation happens a lot in our lives, and most of the time we don't even know it. Did you ever wonder why the cashier at the grocery store was in such a bad mood? Maybe she just got a call that someone close to her was admitted to the hospital. Maybe she was up all night taking care of a child that has cancer or some other life-threatening disease. Or maybe the Department of Human Services took her children from her home because her spouse or boyfriend was abusing them. We never know what is going on in someone else's life. That person who seems to be road raging may have gotten an emergency phone call that his wife or child is very sick. Or a cranky coworker might have just gotten notice that his/her home was being foreclosed. The truth is, everyone is who they are as a result of what has or is currently happening in their lives. Many times we react to others based on what we are feeling. We become cranky when we are upset and take it out on others we are around, but we get angry with them when they do the same to us.

Seeing others' perspectives can sometimes totally change the way we think and act. When people are upset and cranky, the last thing they need is to be confronted by someone who doesn't like their attitude. That only makes matters worse. The Bible tells us in 1 Thessalonians 5:15, *"Make sure that nobody pays back wrong for wrong, but always try to be kind to each other and to everyone else."* If we will respond to angry people in pleasant ways, there is a good chance they will change their attitude, at least for that moment. Sometimes it takes a kind word for others to realize that they are being ugly.

Seeing others' perspectives works right along with unrealistic expectations. When we have our own expectations of others, we cannot see their perspective at all. All we can see is what we are wanting or needing. Letting go of the expectations will help us to see what others are experiencing. We expect customer service people to be nice. When they aren't, we get upset because they are not meeting our expectations of them. Although our expectations may be justified (customer service people are paid to serve the customer, which includes being pleasant to them), the people who work in those positions are just as human as we are—they have lives outside of the job. As we all know, it is very difficult to leave personal problems at home. Our problems are a part of who we are, and leaving them someplace else is almost impossible. Yes, we can learn not to let them affect us as much, but that is a learned process that many people have never developed. So, for them, they carry their personal stuff to work and then take it out on those around them. Wrong or right, it is the truth. So our choice, in order to help us maintain our anger in an appropriate way, is to try to somewhat understand what they might be experiencing. People don't usually act mean for no reason. There is almost always a root problem. So imagining what that problem could possibly be can help us to respond in a kind manner. The more we can imagine, the more capable we can be for compassion.

Another way to try to see others' perspectives is to try for a minute to put yourself in their shoes. Imagine what it would be like, considering what you are personally experiencing in your life, to be where they are right now. What if you were just told that someone you are close to has a major medical problem, then you had to go to work as a clerk at a grocery store where you are expected to smile and be pleasant to all the customers? Suppose you had already used up all your paid time off because of sick kids, and if you missed another day at work, you would be fired. You have no choice, regardless of what information you have just been told; you have to go to work. How would you feel? It is impossible to exactly understand or feel what others feel, but imagining yourself in their situation can help you glance into their perspective.

Learning to imagine others' perspectives has made shopping a much more pleasant activity for me. When I find myself in line waiting for a slow, cranky clerk, I will begin to imagine. I watch nonverbal communication (actions). I watch facial expressions and body movements to see what they convey. I begin to imagine what their life is like. I wonder if they are students, parents, grandparents, or if they are single. I let my mind go as wild as it wants. Then, when it becomes my turn to be checked out, I can start a pleasant conversation with them based on my imagination, not on the way they are acting. Ephesians 4:32 tells us to be *"kind and compassionate to one another"* [1]. This definitely helps me to be more compassionate. It can also be quite fun. Sometimes people will actually begin to open up when I do this. They will discuss what is going on in their lives. It may even give me the opportunity to talk about Jesus. This also helps me if I, too, am having a bad day. I can use this to begin to get my perspective straight, therefore helping me adjust my attitude.

We can be so judgmental toward other people that we are blind to any type of compassion. We say things to ourselves like, *"She shouldn't be acting like that,"* or *"I can't believe that person is being so rude,"* and we get so offended by what they are doing or saying that we can't find compassion. We have to take a step away from what they are actually doing and/or saying to self-talk to ourselves about how we will act toward this person. Again, self-talk is the way to get past offenses. We can self-talk ourselves into having compassion for others, even someone that is being a jerk to us.

We also can be so blinded by our own perspective that we cannot possibly see anyone else's. We can believe so strongly about our view that we set up barriers to keep any other perspective out. Our circumstances can be so overwhelming at times that we have a hard time separating them from what others are experiencing. We get so involved in our own lives that we don't care what others are going through. The Bible tells us in 1 Peter 3:8–9, *"Finally, all of you, live in harmony with one another, be sympathetic. Love as brothers, be compassionate and humble. Do not repay evil with evil or insult with insult, but with blessing, because to this you were called so that you may inherit a blessing."* Our responsibility is to try to live in harmony with others. That scripture doesn't say, *"Unless you are going through too much stuff yourself."* It says to live in harmony and be sympathetic.

Again, self-talk. When your circumstances seem so overwhelming that you cannot handle them, then you face someone else that isn't being nice, stop for a second and self-talk. Remember that hurting people hurt people. Our natural response is to snap back when someone snaps at us. We yell when someone else yells. We are rude when others are rude. But this goes against what the Bible teaches. If we want God to bless us in our difficult circumstances, we need to learn to bless others in theirs. Also, it always helps me to help others. If I am having a hard time with something, and then I am confronted with someone else's circumstances, usually mine don't seem so bad. I can turn my energies and compassion toward them and forget about mine for a while, and that feels good. This is also a good way to help me stop worrying about my circumstances. How can I worry about them if I'm not thinking about them?

Sometimes we over-identify with others' issues. We see a customer and a clerk having a disagreement, and we will identify (because of our past experiences) with one or the other of them. We will get angry for them, thinking in our minds that the other person is wrong. Here, we can start self-talking in a negative way: *"If I was that person, I would...."* We begin to carry our hurts into their circumstances. I have even seen people get into the middle of the others' argument as a result or yell at the clerk when it is their turn to be checked out.

Have you ever thought about praying for someone who is being rude, mean, or ugly? Sometimes when I am standing in line waiting and I see others being hateful to each other, I pray for them. I pray for God to bless them and to help them through whatever their difficult circumstances are. I ask God to show himself to them, especially if they aren't believers. I ask him to give them peace and to replace their anger with joy. Again, I am taking my thoughts off of my own circumstances and focusing on others'. I am having compassion for them through my prayers. This helps me to be nice to them when I get to the front of the line. I will start the conversation by saying something like, *"Are you having a bad day?"* Then I will let them know it is okay with me if they take a second to calm down, that I'm not in a hurry, even if I am. I'm not talking about lying; I'm talking about giving them a break. I have found that they end up working faster and more efficiently when I do this. It helps them to get their mind off of what just happened. I guess I have worked in customer service situations enough in my past that I understand a little of what they experience.

I use customer service representatives a lot for illustrations in this chapter, but the same principles work in any situation where the person you are dealing with is being rude in some way. It even works with people who are road raging. When we learn to self-talk, we can learn not to get offended at what others are doing and learn to be compassionate and understanding toward them instead. The Bible also tells us that *"a gentle answer turns away wrath, but a harsh word stirs up anger"* (Proverbs 15:1). This is basically saying that when we answer ugliness with niceness, we will melt the person's heart, but if we react to ugliness with our own anger, we just cause more anger. Proverbs 25:21–22 tells us, *"If your enemy is hungry, give him food to eat; if he is thirsty, give him water to drink. In doing so you will heap burning coals on his head, and the Lord will reward you."* God rewards niceness. He likes to see us bless others, especially when they are being mean to us. When we heap burning coals on the heads of our enemies, we are basically showing them the niceness of God. After we walk away, they will feel bad about their actions. Maybe, as a result, they will come to know Jesus. Can you imagine how it would feel if someone dumped burning coals on your head? Even after the coals are removed, the burn is still there. That is how effective being positive to a negative person can be—it can leave afterthoughts for a long time.

I know some of you are probably thinking that people don't deserve that kind of niceness. It's called grace. Grace is undeserved favor. We don't deserve the grace God gives us either, but He continues to give it to us daily. Also, even though those people don't deserve your grace, you deserve it for yourself. It is much like forgiveness. The people we forgive many times don't deserve our forgiveness. But if we don't forgive them, we are the ones who end up suffering. When we carry unforgiveness in our hearts, we keep anger there too. We hold grudges, and we dwell on how to get even. The other person goes on with his life as if nothing is wrong while we are torn up inside.

If we are harsh when others are ugly, we then carry the shame of not giving grace. Then the enemy comes in and lays a huge guilt trip on us. If we don't recognize it, we can destroy ourselves with this unending cycle. We can stop the cycle by just being nice.

And last, if not least, the golden rule, *"Do unto others the way you would have them do unto you"* (Matthew 7:12, not the way they are doing unto you!

CHAPTER 11
Goal Setting

During my bachelor's program, I learned a lot about setting goals. I had to. I had not been in school since I graduated from high school seventeen years earlier. Starting college was a major accomplishment for me. But it quickly became overwhelming. The only thing I had studied since high school was the Bible. I was a wife, stay-at-home mom, soccer coach, PTA officer, and Bible study leader. Even though I had my own home-based business, I had never done anything like going to college. I enjoyed my Bible classes, but English, history, college math, and science freaked me out. After the first few weeks of college, I was all ready to give up.

Before enrollment, I had to take the ACT test for class placement. I scored a 28 in English. That meant I received an ACT credit for English Comp 1, and I was placed in the English Comp 2 class. Supposedly, I knew enough about English that I wasn't required to take the first class. The truth was, I knew nothing about English. I didn't know a verb from an adverb. I talked to my

English teacher, and she told me that it was not because of the specifics of English that I scored high on the ACT, it was because of life experience. I had written and read enough to know how things were supposed to sound. She told me not to worry, that I would do fine. Easy for her to say, she was the teacher! And to top it off, rumor was that she was the most difficult teacher in the school. I was freaking out inside.

My advisor offered a *"learning to study"* seminar several weeks after school started. I decided I had better take this class if I ever hoped to make it through college. It was a life-changing class for me. First of all, I found out that my advisor was a wonderful man and a dedicated professor who wanted to help me as much as I would allow him to (if you are reading this, Dr. Hargett, thank you!). Secondly, I learned something of great value that I will use the rest of my life—goal setting. I had some huge goals in front of me that were overwhelming. Math was the big one. I barely made it through math in high school, much less college. It wasn't until much later, when I learned that I have ADD, that I understood why I had such a problem with math. In this class of goal setting, I learned that we tend to set big, unreasonable, sometimes unrealistic goals for ourselves, and by doing so we basically set ourselves up for failure. Learning to set small, reasonable goals changed my life.

Let me explain this in a simple way. Everyone has either struggled with a weight problem or knows someone who has. The tendency for people wanting to lose weight is to set a goal of how many total pounds they want to lose, let's say fifty pounds. Then they start setting goals within that one: walk every day, workout at the gym five times a week, limit calorie intake to 1000 calories a day, limit fat gram intake to under twenty grams a day, no sugar, only protein or grapefruit, etc. The first day, the second day, and maybe even the third day, they do great. Then the fourth day they wake up hungry and hurting. This is where compromise starts. They begin justifying in their minds, I don't think I will go to the gym today. I am too sore. I will just eat this one time. I am really hungry. Does this sound familiar? It isn't very long before they totally give up, throw in the towel, and say, "*I've failed again.*" This can cause a great deal of stress and anger, mostly because the person really wants to lose weight.

When goals are unsuccessfully met on a continuing basis, we become disappointed with ourselves. This can instill within us not only a sense of failure, but also promote low self-esteem and low self-confidence. The more this happens, the less we tend to want to try. It is good to fail sometimes. Some of the greatest success stories in our history began as failures. But if failure seems like a habit, it becomes so discouraging that we lose hope of anything ever being successful and we quit trying.

Anger at ourselves is one of the hardest issues to overcome. We have a difficult time forgiving ourselves; therefore, we stay angry. Many times the anger is really unjustified. We get angry at ourselves for making mistakes, for forgetting something important, for falling short of our goals, and for many other things that we would gladly forgive others for. I have learned to self-talk myself through this kind of anger. I try to think about how I would feel if someone else did the same thing to me that I was angry at myself for, and they were repentant. Then I imagine how I would treat them. I am a very compassionate person. I cannot stay angry at someone who truly voices their apology. So why shouldn't I be compassionate to myself?

Now let's discuss some different goals that could be set for the weight-loss scenario previously discussed. We'll use, for example, Jenny. She is the one wanting to lose fifty pounds. The main goal, obviously, is to lose weight. But, within that main goal, she needs to set some small, reasonable goals that can be more quickly attained. First, she will want to think about what the core reason for her wanting to lose weight is. In her case, it is for health reasons. After discussing this with her doctor, she decides to cut her intake of fat grams down from the normal of seventy-five to one hundred grams a day to below fifty grams a day. (It is always a good idea to check with your doctor before going on a diet, especially when the weight loss is related to health issues.) Jenny has now set her first goal.

Simple, huh? Jenny will try to maintain that goal of below fifty grams per day for at least a week, maybe two. She can very gradually reduce her fat intake until she reaches the doctor's recommended daily intake. She should reward herself for maintaining below fifty grams per day on a consistent basis for at least a week. Then, if her doctor's recommendation is twenty grams per day, she can reward herself each time she drops another ten grams. The rewards need to be something that is good for her, specifically. I like to do things like rent a love story, take a long hot bath by candlelight with worship music playing, go to a movie or shopping (if I have any money), or go to lunch with a friend. The rewards need to be something she wouldn't have or do otherwise, so they are really rewards. Rewarding herself gives her a sense of accomplishment and will help build self-esteem and confidence. She will feel good about the accomplishment, and that will encourage her to do more.

It would be okay for Jenny to set other small, reasonable goals to work on while she is accomplishing her goal of reducing her intake of fat grams, if she doesn't overdo it. For example, she could start with a goal of walking a couple of blocks once or twice a week. Then she could gradually build to three or four days a week, and so on. She could then build her distance to several blocks and eventually to a mile. (Again, it would be wise for Jenny to check with her doctor before beginning any exercise regimen.)

Next she could begin counting calories or working out at the gym, doing so in a slow, gradual process and rewarding herself at predetermined times along the way. It may seem like this process of losing weight will take forever, but it takes even longer when the goals are unattainable, therefore relinquished. Continuously starting and stopping the process of losing weight can go on for years without success and can sometimes cause weight gain instead of loss. Starting with small, reasonable goals and gradually building upward may seem like it is a long process, but in reality, it accomplishes much more than just the weight loss.

Another important thing to know about setting small goals is that if you don't accomplish one of them, you don't have to "*throw in the towel*" of the larger goal you are working toward. If you have a bad day, you write it off as a bad day, and you pick up the next day with where you left off. One bad day does not eradicate all the other good days and goals you have accomplished up to that point.

This process of goal setting can be used in many areas of our lives, such as quitting smoking, going to college, looking for a job, and cleaning house. Quitting smoking is an easy one to set these types of goals with. First, start with slowly cutting down how much you smoke. Cut down one or two cigarettes every few days, or even once a week until you have cut your daily intake in half. Then reward yourself. Rewards for quitting smoking are easier because you can save the money you have been spending on cigarettes and use that toward the rewards—double accomplishment.

Next, begin the process of breaking the habit by changing the times and places you smoke. If you are used to smoking inside, only smoke outside. If you are used to smoking after a meal, don't do it anymore.

Change the hand you smoke with. Don't buy cartons, and change brands with every pack you buy. Don't smoke generic brands because they contain other products you can become addicted to besides the nicotine. Then you have those addictions to deal with also. Chew gum or chew on a straw between cigarettes. If you feel it necessary, ask your doctor to prescribe one of the new smoking-cessation drugs or purchase an over-the-counter one. There are some very good, effective products on the market today.

Receiving the information I did from the studying seminar, along with other information I learned about the same topic throughout my college education, helped me successfully make it through college. If I found out during the first week of a semester that I had a big project or a term paper due at the end of a semester, I would make a timeline. Using a sixteen-week term, I would exclude the first and last three weeks of school in my timeline. It is really hard to get motivated the first week of class. It is enough to just get organized. I didn't include the last three weeks in case of unseen circumstances that might come up during the semester, like sickness. So I would lay out on a piece of paper a timeline with twelve weeks on it. Then I would divide my project by twelve and set a goal to accomplish one twelfth of the project each week.

It worked great. I was never late on a single project, very seldom worked until the last night, and almost always finished early by a week or so. The grade was the reward! Also, there were days, especially in my bachelor's program, where I had to set daily goals because I had so much going on. Being a wife, mother, employee, student, and church volunteer, there were times I had too much on my plate. I would make a list the night before of what I would like to accomplish the next day. I would check off the list as I completed a task. Without daily goals, I could have easily become overwhelmed and given up on everything, then been really angry at myself for allowing it to happen. Doing things the way I did, I graduated third in my class with a 3.91 grade point average (summa cum laude). That was quite an accomplishment for someone who barely graduated high school because of bad grades.

Let's look at some of the other areas where you can set goals to accomplish a task. When looking for a new job, make out a list of all the things you can do, like writing or updating your résumé, developing a list of contacts in your field of expertise, and decide how many résumés and/or interviews you would like to have each week. All of these things can be put in goal form, written out on a timeline, and highlighted as they are completed. This will again give you a personal sense of accomplishment.

I don't know very many people who really like to clean house, especially major jobs like spring cleaning. I also know some people who have never been good housekeepers but would like to be. The thought of cleaning a whole house at once, especially if it is really messy, can prevent you from even starting. Make a list. Start with the easiest room, or maybe a drawer or closet. Work on one small project at a time and reward yourself each time you get one area cleaned. Don't allow yourself to get caught up in going from one room to another finding other stuff that needs to be done.

When my husband and I clean the garage, we only clean the garage. If there are things in the garage that need to be put away in the house, we set those aside. We don't go right then and put them where they belong because it is too easy to get distracted by something else that needs to be done in that room. After we clean the garage, we work on the stack of household items we put aside, one at a time. Then, if the place we are putting things needs cleaning, we can decide whether to do it then or just leave that item there with the rest of the mess until the right time comes for working on that project. That stack might sit there for a few days until we have the time to put it all away. But this way we don't become overwhelmed with too much at once.

If you are one of those types of people who have a hard time getting organized, develop a timeline, make lists, and write out your goals. Developing them visually will help you keep them. Put them someplace where you can constantly see them and mark the ones you accomplish with a bright highlighter.

The reason I am giving so many details about setting goals is that I feel goal setting is essential to anger management. You see, when I would fail at something, I would not only get angry at myself, but I would take my anger out on others around me. By setting small, reasonable, attainable goals, I no longer fail at the big stuff. I slowly work toward what I want to accomplish until the project is complete. This reduces my list of things I get angry about by one more item.

The Bible tells us that Paul had goals. He says in Philippians 3:14 that he is pressing on toward the goal to win the prize for which God has called him heavenward in Christ Jesus[1]. Then in Acts 20:24, he says, "*I consider my life worth nothing to me, if only I may finish the race and complete the task the Lord Jesus has given me—the task of testifying to the gospel of God's grace.*" Seeing that Paul set goals for himself and that he pressed forward toward accomplishing them encourages me. It shows me that goal setting is a good thing. The Lord gives us tasks to complete just as He gave them to Paul. Those tasks are different for each of us. One is called to be a mother, another a pastor, another an employee. In order for us to accomplish those tasks, and do them well, we must not become overwhelmed by them. Reasonable goal setting will not only help us complete those things we want to do for ourselves, it will also help us accomplish the tasks Jesus has set before us.

CHAPTER 12
Are You Angry with God?

The Bible tells us in James 1:2–4 to, "*Consider it pure joy, my brothers, whenever you face trials of many kinds, because you know that the testing of your faith develops perseverance. Perseverance must finish its work so that you may be mature and complete, not lacking anything.*" This can be a very difficult scripture for us to understand and an even harder one to apply. How can we consider it joy when we are going through trials? Trials are hard, and we get hurt. One day as I was preparing a lesson for an anger management session I was going to teach at church, the Lord revealed to me an incredible truth about this scripture and about my anger toward him. In this chapter I will share that truth with you.

For as long as I can remember, I have prayed for the Lord's will in my life. I have done so even when it was a difficult prayer to pray. One time I really wanted a recently developed position in my church. I talked to the people I needed to, and everything was set to go. A few days before I was supposed to start working, I prayed and asked God if it was not His will for me to take this position, for Him to stop it. I did not want to start something His hand was not in. That was a hard prayer for me to pray because I really wanted this job. But I wanted God's will more. It wasn't too long after that prayer that I received a phone call from the pastor's wife. She told me that they (the people in charge of the project) had decided not to fill that position at that time. The other people involved were going to cover it. I knew immediately that the Lord had stopped me from getting involved in that project because it wasn't His will for me at that time, and I had a peace in knowing that.

As Christians, we are taught through God's Word to pray for His will. The prayer Jesus gave us as the very foundation for our prayer life supports it:

This, then, is how you should pray: Our Father in heaven, hallowed be your name, your kingdom come, your will be done on earth as it is in heaven. Give us today our daily bread. Forgive us our debts, as we also have forgiven our debtors. And lead us not into temptation, but deliver us from the evil one.
Matthew 6:9–13

See that middle scripture? It says, "*Your will be done.*" We, as Christians, pray for the Father's will in our lives. As we pray for God's will, we trust that He will answer that prayer. Then trials come. The scripture previously mentioned in James tells us why we go through trials: "*the testing of our faith develops perseverance*" [1]. Through perseverance, we mature in our Christian walk. Our faith grows through trials and so does our maturity. So God allows us to go through trials because He wants us to grow. We pray for God's will, God's will is for us to grow, but we get mad at Him when He allows things to happen that we don't like.

I know so many people who are, or have been, angry with God for bad things that have happened in their lives. I have been angry with God many times in the past. I have asked Him for things and haven't gotten them and then gotten angry at Him for not providing for me the way I thought He should. Or I would get angry at Him when life would throw me a difficult blow, knowing that He could easily fix my situation and he wasn't. The only way we are going to grow in our faith is for our faith to be tested. If God erased every difficult circumstance for us, our faith would not mature. It is going through those circumstances that we grow.

One time, about fifteen years ago, Brad and I wanted to buy the house we were renting. The owner filed bankruptcy, and the bank foreclosed on it. Since we were already living in it, the house was offered to us first. We tried everything we could to purchase the house, but we could not qualify for it. This process of us trying to buy the house lasted about three months. When we received the final notice that we were not going to be able to buy it and we had five days to get out, I was devastated. I remember standing in the shower, crying my eyes out and yelling at God because he did not give us this home. I didn't want to move. I was so hurt and angry. It took everything I had to pack all our stuff and move.

We moved to another rent house one block away. I hated it. I didn't want to be there. I wanted my house, the other one. Because we were so close, and because we still had several friends on that street, I had to see the house all the time. Every time I would drive by it, I would feel that sharp pain inside. One day I saw someone moving into it. My heart broke even more. I couldn't believe that God did this to me.

Gradually, over time, the pain lessened, and it didn't bother me so much to drive by it. About a year later, I was talking to the neighbor who lived next door. She asked me if I had heard what happened with the house.

Surprised, I said *"No, what?"* She informed me that there were a ton of major plumbing and electrical problems, and the new owners couldn't afford to fix them, so they packed up and moved out. Wow! I had never thought about that aspect of it before. If we would have owned that house, it would have been us facing those repairs, and we, too, could not have afforded them. What I realized is that God actually saved us from losing a home instead of giving us one that would have been a lot of trouble and expense. We may never know all the reasons God allows or does not allow us to face difficult circumstances. This lesson taught me that God knows best.

I also want to share with you how my husband learned the same lesson. The house wasn't that big of a deal to him. A house is a house. He didn't care if we were in that house or a block over. But a job is a major thing to him. His heart's desire was to be an air traffic controller (ATC). In 1987, he started at the Mike Monroney ATC Training Center in Oklahoma City. We were actually living in Arlington, Texas, at the time, so he had to travel to OKC and stay with my parents while he went to school. About two weeks after he started class, the boys and I were scheduled to drive to OKC to be with him for the weekend. I had to do a couple of things before the time for us to leave, so I left the boys at home to run my errands.

I was driving down the street and was pulled over by a policeman for a random traffic check. No big deal, I thought. He went back to his car and did a routine search on my driver's license. He then came back to my car and told me there was a warrant out for my arrest. I was shocked! He said it was for an old bogus check charge from several years earlier in Oklahoma City. I found out later that when we left OKC to move to Texas, we didn't leave enough money in our checking account for a check to clear. A felony was sixty dollars at that time; the check was for sixty-four. Because I had not covered the check, the warrant was issued. We left forwarding addresses and all the stuff we were supposed to do when we moved, so we had no idea why I had not received notification. But, the truth is, back then, we lived life pretty much on the edge. We took a lot of chances we shouldn't have, and it was really amazing that we hadn't been caught yet. Needless to say, I was handcuffed, arrested, and taken to the city police station.

ATC school was one of the hardest schools in the world to pass. It took time, patience, and lots of concentration. Brad is a very intelligent person, and under normal circumstances it would have been a struggle for him to pass that school. Now his wife was in jail hundreds of miles away, his children were at home alone by themselves (they were about six and nine at the time), and he could do nothing about it. To make a long story short, they refused bail and told me they wanted me extradited back to OKC. They told me I would have to stay in jail until they got a driver to transport me back to Oklahoma. Brad was freaking out. By the grace and blessings of God, three days later they let me out. I was to go directly to OKC and stay there until my court date, which was a couple of weeks away. Brad was struggling with school already because of the circumstances. Now the boys and I had to stay there with them him. There was no peace and quiet, no concentration. He struggled through the whole course, and on the last day, he failed by only a few points. He was devastated. He got angry with God. How could a God, who loves His children as much as He says in His Word, allow this to happen? Brad tried for over a year to get accepted back into the academy but to no avail. His destiny was not to be a controller. This was very difficult for him to deal with, and as a result, a deep-seated anger was rooted in his heart. Now, I know this is a sad story and it seems very unfair, but God does take those things that the enemy meant for bad and He turns them around for our good (Romans 8:28)[2].

Brad always kept ATC in his heart. He began to have a yearning to write a computer game of ATC simulation. At the time he entered the academy, he was just learning how to write computer programs, and every so often he would mess around with it. It wasn't until years later, in 1999, that his dream started to become a reality. He found a publisher who was willing to front the money for him to develop his game, as well as mass produce and distribute the game to worldwide retail and wholesalers. He was able to quit his regular job and devote all his time to writing this program. On January 16, 2001, his game was published. The revenue from the sales of this software supported us for over 15 years! We don't know why God allowed things the way He did. We may never know. But God gave Brad the desires of his heart, in His perfect timing.

The enemy knows each of our weakest areas and, therefore, attacks us in them—that's the trial. When we overcome, we become stronger in that area. The stronger we become, the more the enemy is defeated. For example, the enemy used to attack me in the area of rejection every day. My life was a constant struggle of rejections with my husband, my kids, my friends, and my family. As soon as I would get past one circumstance, something else would happen. I went through a lot of rejection trials before I learned how to recognize and overcome them. Even though he still attacks in that area sometimes, it isn't near as often, nor am I affected near as much. When we don't learn from a trial, we stay weak in that area. The enemy continues to attack and we continue to get hurt. As a result, many of us stay mad at God; therefore, we don't grow.

We will go through the same trials over and over until we learn whatever lesson it is God wants us to learn. Now, I don't believe God causes bad things to happen. James 1:3 says, *"When tempted, no one should say 'God is tempting me.' For God cannot be tempted by evil, nor does He tempt anyone."* Then Peter tells us in 2 Peter 2:9, *"The Lord knows how to rescue godly men from trials."* Trials are temptations for us to get angry. Whether it is at God, the situation, the others involved, or the world in general, it is common practice to be, or to get, angry when going through trials.

I like the saying that goes something like this: *"When life throws you a lemon, make lemonade."* I love lemonade! Trials are opportunities for God to do something good in our lives. It is all in how you choose to look at it. Is your glass half-empty or half-full? Positive or negative attitudes can make all the difference in the world when going through trials. Positive attitudes can reflect the trust you have in God. Remember that old faithful chapter of Psalm 23? Verse 4 says, *"Even though I walk through the valley of the shadow of death, I will fear no evil, for you are with me; your rod and your staff, they comfort me"*. It does not say, *"Even though I stay in the valley"*; it says, *"walk through."* That means we aren't going to stay there, but while we are there, God will comfort us, if we allow Him to.

When it feels like nothing else could go wrong, when things keep piling on each other, and when I feel overwhelmed, I have learned to laugh. Proverbs 17:22 says, *"A merry heart does good like a medicine."* This is my favorite scripture in the Bible. A merry heart reflects a merry attitude, and I believe it is a choice. 1st Corinthians 10:13 says, *"No temptation has seized you except what is common to man. And God is faithful; He will not let you be tempted beyond what you can bear. But when you are tempted, He will also provide a way out so that you can stand up under it."* Remember, trials are temptations not to trust God. He promises us here that He will never allow us to be tempted more than what He gives us the ability to overcome, with His help. The problem is, we try to do it on our own, instead of trusting God. We get mad at Him because trials are difficult and we don't want to go through them. But without them, we will never grow, and therefore, we will never have God's will perfected in our lives.

The Bible also tells us that the Lord will strengthen and protect us from the evil one [3], and it says that no weapon the enemy sends against us will conquer us[4]. Here, again, is where self-talk comes in. Learning to self-talk scriptures is the way to overcome trials. Confessing the scriptures over our lives will help build our faith. We speak those things that are not as though they are[5], and we walk by faith, not by sight[6]. We can become stronger in trials by self-talking these scriptures along with making positive statements like, *"God will get me through this. He will not give me more than I can handle. He is in control, so I don't have to be. I'm trusting Him in this situation."*

Of course, we also have to spend time in prayer. We need to praise Him for our past victories and for the one He is currently taking us through. We also need to worship Him in the midst of the battle. Matthew 6:33–34 says, *"But seek first His kingdom and His righteousness, and all these things will be given to you as well. Therefore do not worry about tomorrow, for tomorrow will worry about itself. Each day has enough trouble of its own."* When we offer God praise and we worship Him in the midst of troubles, we are seeking Him instead of worrying about our circumstances.

Jesus also went through trials. Matthew chapter 4 tells the story about Jesus being tempted by the enemy after forty days alone in the wilderness. Instead of giving in to the temptations the enemy offered him, Jesus turned to God and used His words to defeat the enemy. Second Peter 1:3–4 tells us that God has given us everything we need for life and godliness. It also says that through the promises God has given us, we can escape the corruption of this world[7]. God has provided for us everything we need to overcome the trials of this world. All we have to do is learn to apply them to our lives.

When you pray for God's will for your life, then trials come along, trust God in them, knowing that He is allowing them to happen so that you will grow in Him, therefore perfecting His will for your life. Instead of getting angry at God for the trials you face, trust Him in them. Embrace trials, knowing there is a reason you are going through them, and the reason is ultimately for your good.

James 1:12 says,

"Blessed is the man who perseveres under trial, because when he has stood the test, he will receive the crown of life that God promised to those who love Him."

How can we get angry at God for allowing trials in our lives, when in actuality, we asked for them by praying for God's will? If we really trust God, we won't get angry at Him. This is how we can *"consider it joy"* when we are going through trials. The joy comes when we realize that God is working for our good. As we trust Him, He will deliver us through the difficult circumstances, stronger than ever, defeating the enemy one more time.

CHAPTER 13
Fair Fighting

One of the first things I do when I begin counseling with couples is to help them develop a set of fair-fighting rules. These are rules for them to agree to use when disagreements arise. Many couples who come to counseling think they are not supposed to fight, and they want me to teach them how to communicate without fighting. I always refer them to the old saying, "*No pain, no gain.*" Without disagreements, the relationship can't grow. Relationships are about getting to know each other. Since each person was raised in different environments with different parents and with different sets of rules and values, there will be disagreements. So instead of trying to "*not fight,*" I encourage them to learn to fight fairly.

I want to remind you that the Bible does not tell us not to get angry. It says that in your anger you are not to sin[1]. Agreeing on rules to keep when a fight occurs will help a couple learn how to keep their anger under control and, therefore, not sin. Within that statement lies the basic rule of fair fighting: agreeing to keep the rules. If a couple really wants a relationship to work, they must keep these rules no matter what. They must agree that one will not ignore the other when the rules are mentioned. They must also both agree to not get angry (or more angry) at the other person for reminding him or her about the rules.

The first thing I talk with couples about it is the word divorce. If two people want to make a marriage work, they have to totally remove the word divorce from their vocabulary. It cannot be used as a threat or an alternative to working through problems. If the word does not exist, it cannot happen. Brad and I have never discussed divorce as an option to our problems. We have always known that we would have to figure out some way to work out whatever problem we were facing, because we would never divorce. Couples getting married today know that if it doesn't work, they can get a divorce. How easy is that? Why try to work things out when it is easier to just divorce. I encourage young couples getting married in the same way. Do not ever use divorce as an alternative to solving problems. If you don't bring it up, it won't happen. It isn't an option.

The next rule I discuss with couples is about name-calling. Brad and I have been married now for more than forty two years. In that time I can proudly say that neither of us has ever called each other a name out of anger. We have joking pet names we call each other when we are playing around (because he is a dork!) but never a bad name and never out of anger. Names stick in people's minds. Even if there is an apology, a person will later remember that his or her spouse had called them something ugly. In the back of their minds they will always wonder if their spouse really feels that way.

Let me give you an example. This story is about a newly married couple that in the midst of a fight, the husband called the wife an ugly name. Twenty or so years later, the couple is in their pastor's office discussing some financial issues. The pastor and the husband are talking about a certain topic when the pastor turns to the wife and asks her what she thinks. Because of the ugly name her husband had called her years earlier, she stated that her opinion didn't matter. That name had caused a deep wound that she carried for many years. Who knows how many times she had dwelled on him calling her that during their marriage. Name-calling can hurt very deeply and last a long time, and besides all that, it is sin. Remember, in your anger, do not sin[2]. So the first rule is no name calling.

The next thing we discuss is forgiveness. Without forgiveness of past issues, it is impossible for a relationship to move forward. Do you remember in Chapter 3, I gave the illustration about the pond? If not, now is a good time to go back and read it. Those old issues will rise up with the storms. In relationships, there are storms. So forgiveness is essential for successful relationships. This is a good place to bring up love. First Corinthians 13:4–8 says,

Love is patient, love is kind. It does not envy, it does not boast, it is not proud. It is not rude, it is not self-seeking, it is not easily angered, it keeps no record of wrongs. Love does not delight in evil but rejoices with the truth. It always protects, always trusts, always hopes, always perseveres. Love never fails.

Forgiveness means we are able to live the middle part of those verses, which says love "*keeps no record of wrongs.*" Yes, there will be times when one spouse hurts another. But if we really love each other, we will forgive.

If the relationship of the couple I am working with is fairly healthy and there is no violence, here's one thing that I suggest couples do: Choose a night when you can be alone—uninterrupted. Make sure it is a time when you can find a sitter for the children. Shut off all of your digital devices (cellphone, iPad, TV, etc). Find a place in your home that is comfortable. A suggestion is the floor of your bedroom. Dim the lights or shut them off and use candles. Put a blanket on the floor and the two of you sit together on it. Then begin talking. Talk about everything that has ever happened between the two of you where there were offenses. Be honest. Don't keep secrets. Talk about everything. Get it all out. Now remember, this is not a time to fight—it is a time to discuss. If a fight starts, end the session. This is a time for healing, not for causing more wounds. Use "*I*" statements instead of "*you*" statements ("*I feel*" and "*I felt*" instead of "*you made me feel*"). Discuss one topic at a time, and don't blame. Listen to each other's feelings and accept responsibility. Apologize. Forgive. Use this evening to put an end to the past. From this point forward, you will have a new life together. This is a new beginning. The past is forgiven, and the future holds hope.

If the session had to end because a fight started or if the relationship is not stable or healthy enough for this type of interaction, I do this with the couple in my office. It may take a few sessions, but this is an essential part of setting fair-fighting rules and for the start of making a relationship work. I also do this with couples during premarital counseling. I believe it is the best way to start a marriage—get the past settled and start new.

With this accomplished, we go on to discuss and establish fair-fighting rules. The next one on the list is two parts. The first part is the rule of discussing one topic at a time. The second part is to not bring up the past. What happens in most fights is the couple will have a simple disagreement. With that usually come additional topics. One person will say something like, "*Well, you did so and so the other day,*" to justify what they did. Then a second topic comes into the discussion.

The other spouse will then say something like, "*Yeah, but remember when you...*" I'm sure you can already see the reason for the forgiveness session before the actual rule setting. If the past is forgiven, it cannot be used again; therefore, it cannot be brought up. If a couple can stick to this rule, they can many times settle the argument easily at this point. If there is no past, or other issues to discuss, there isn't as much to argue about. But if another issue comes up that needs to be discussed, put that it for another session.

When there is a disagreement, listen to what the other person is saying. Take the time and really listen. Many times a discussion gets heated when one person isn't really listening or he or she misinterpret what the other person is trying to say. I know that most of the big fights Brad and I have gotten into have been as a result of one of us misunderstanding what the other one said. Then there is an offense. Now, when Brad and I have a disagreement and he says something that I instantly feel offended about, I will immediately respond by saying something like, "*Ouch!*" and I will tell him what I thought he said. Then he will apologize for the offense and say that wasn't what he was trying to say. He will then reword it until we both understand what he is trying to communicate.

When we get offended, we get angry and tend to lash back. But usually, it wasn't our partner's intention to offend. He or she was just trying to get their point across, and it just came out as offensive. Again, it is important to remember that we can always choose to not get offended. But if that is too difficult at the time, stop the discussion by speaking your feelings instead of getting angry at the offense. Even if you have to restate what you are trying to say several times, it is worth it to not offend.

Take ownership of your own feelings. Don't blame your spouse for the way you feel. You choose the way you will act or react to what he or she says. Blaming just causes more anger because it puts the other person on the defense. That is why it is important to use *"I"* statements instead of *"you"* statements.

Sometimes, out of anger, a spouse will say something that is offensive and is intended to be offensive. What do you do then? Discuss why he or she feels it is important to offend. Why does he or she feel like offending the partner will make the situation better? Together, see if you can figure out a way to say what needs to be said without it being offensive. (This is also a great thing to do between teenagers and parents.) Remember, we are trying to work on improving the relationship, improving the communication skills, improving the way we work on disagreements, and working on keeping a marriage together. Purposeful offenses are not an effective way to accomplish this. 1 Corinthians 13 says that love is kind and it does not delight in evil. When we say things that hurt on purpose, that is not kindness nor is it showing love. It is delighting in evil. Here we are again: *"In your anger do not sin."*

Isn't it true that many times when you are fighting you have already figured out what you are going to say before your spouse even completes what he or she is saying? How can we do that if we are really listening to what the other is saying? We live in a microwave society. We want fast food, fast service, fast everything. Our minds are always working at a fast pace. We do this with friends, coworkers, family, and our spouses, and it is really rude. We rarely completely listen to what another person is saying because we are trying to figure out in our own minds how we are going to respond. Make yourself slow and listen long enough to repeat back what the other person is saying.

When we do this in an argument, we don't really hear what the other person is saying. Then, sometimes, we respond with off the wall comments that really don't make sense. We need to take the time to slow our thought process down enough to listen. This takes self-talk. If you find your mind speeding faster than the other person is talking, tell yourself to slow down. Tell yourself to listen to the other person. Take a couple of deep breaths. Consider how it feels when you are talking and you realize the person you are talking to isn't listening.

Do your arguments go on forever and ever? What does that accomplish? The next rule is about setting time limits. Many people I mention this rule to think it is stupid until we actually start discussing it. Isn't it true that after about ten or fifteen minutes, an argument only gets worse, not better? The longer the argument, the higher the anger escalates. And usually, the original topic is long forgotten. After ten or fifteen minutes of discussing a topic, take a break. Take some time apart to think about why you are really angry. Think about the importance of the argument. Is this topic significant enough to continue the discussion, or is it one that you should just apologize and move on from? (See Chapter 15 – Timeouts)

We need to learn to pick our fights based on the merits of the issue. Arguing about insignificant issues is really a waste of time and usually just causes more hurt. Sometimes, spouses want to continue arguments because they want to prove they are right. Being wrong might mean they are less of a person (is there a rejection issue here?). We are not on opposite teams. First Corinthians 13 says that love is not proud nor is it self-seeking. When we argue just to prove we are right we are not showing love. The need to prove our point is prideful, and it is self-seeking (for our own interest instead of the interest of others).

Many times an argument will start because one spouse is tired, sick, or stressed, and the topic of the argument isn't really the issue. Taking a few minutes to separate and think will help clear your mind about what is really going on and what is the best way to re-approach the situation. If and when you realize that you were wrong, admit it and apologize. This can be another pride issue that needs to be stopped. Apologizing is not a sign of weakness but just the opposite—it is a sign of strength. It takes a strong person to recognize they are wrong and then admit it.

When I go to wedding showers and am asked to give suggestions to the bride about how to make a marriage last, I always say compromise. If I were to sum up what makes a good marriage in one word, besides God, I would use the word compromise. Compromise is working toward a solution that is agreeable to both parties involved. In a marriage, each spouse should give equally toward compromises, depending on the importance of the particular issue at hand. If an issue being discussed is really important to one spouse and not really important to the other, then the compromise is easier. But, if the issue is equally important to both spouses, compromise is more difficult. This is the time to get out the paper and pencil. Make a pros and cons list. Each person should write what they think is positive and negative about the possible solutions. Then compare the columns. Many times the best solution will be obvious by comparing lists. Sometimes, however, it might not be so easy. The lists may be close and there may not be an obvious answer. Prayer is the best solution at this point. Not that a couple shouldn't pray before now. But usually, when people are angry, or in the middle of a discussion, the last thing they think about is prayer. Sometimes we have to seek God and His guidance before we can come up with solutions to problems we disagree about. When this happens, it is best not to make any decisions until you both feel you have received a peace from God about the solution.

Sometimes we argue about a topic that there isn't a solution to or that the solution doesn't really matter. That is when we agree to disagree, and that's okay. Paul and Barnabas disagreed. Acts 15:39 tells us that, *"They had such a sharp disagreement that they parted company."* This scripture doesn't say anything about anger, hostility, or bitterness. It just says they parted company. They agreed to disagree, and they went their separate ways. In a marriage, you can't exactly go your separate ways, but you can agree to disagree when the topic being discussed isn't significant.

Here are a few examples of some topics you could agree to disagree about: whether a movie was good or not; what someone else said or didn't say; where you're going to eat lunch ; who's turn it is to cook, clean, or wash the car; the exact name of the color of something; etc. Reading these topics may seem really silly to you right now, but I have heard some super arguments over many such things. People will sometimes continue to argue just for the sake of arguing. That is the time to agree to disagree and let it go. It isn't worth possible hurts that could develop when a simple argument turns into an ugly fight.

When trying to agree to a solution, you always need to consider what is best for everyone involved. Try to come to an agreement that will be positive in some way for both people involved. You may decide on several solutions. Then always apologize. Even if you feel like you were not wrong, apologize anyway.

Now, let's recap:

1. No name-calling.
2. Forgive the past.
3. Discuss one topic at a time, and do not bring up the past.
4. Listen to what the other person is saying.

5. Use "*I*" statements instead of "*you*" statements.
6. Restate your point until it is understood.
7. Take ownership of your own feelings.
8. Do not say hurtful things on purpose.
9. Choose not to get offended.
10. After ten to fifteen minutes, take a time-out to think.
11. Don't argue for the sake of proving you are right.
12. Recognize when you are wrong and apologize.
13. Compromise.
14. Sometimes it's okay to disagree.
15. Decide on a solution that is best for everyone involved.
16. Apologize.

You might want to copy the list and hang it on the refrigerator or some place that you will see it often. Occasionally discuss it. See if there are some things you want to add to it or take away from it. Your rules for fair fighting need to fit you and your circumstances. Agree on what would be good rules for the two of you, write those out and post them. That way you are making them more personal for you. Like I said at the beginning of this chapter, this is something I help couples to develop. They are not a set of rules I give them and tell them they have to obey. It is something discussed and worked through so it fits each need personally.

CHAPTER 14
Parenting and Anger

When I was growing up, my only goals in life were to get married and have children. I didn't have a desire to go to college; I barely made it through high school. Therefore, I didn't have a desire for a career. I just wanted to be a good wife and mother, and I thought I could do that. Of course that was before I got married and had kids. The marriage part wasn't so hard, at first. Brad and I were married eight months when I got pregnant with Bradley. Life still wasn't that difficult. There were late and long nights with the baby, who was constantly sick, and of course there were always money problems, but it still wasn't too bad. Then, a little over a year later, we had some kind of lapse of intelligence or something, because we decided Bradley needed a little brother or sister to play with. Almost from the very beginning of the pregnancy with Robert, the problems started. We didn't know it at the time, but we were having typical newly married with children problems, and we were devastated. Our whole world began to fall apart, and we didn't know what to do. See, we were raised in two different environments, we were taught totally different things, and we learned to cope with difficult circumstances differently. We basically led totally different lives up until the time we got married, so we started butting heads.

Brad and I were very young when we got married. As I have said before, I was seventeen, and he had just turned nineteen the month before. With youth comes immaturity, but since we were still teenagers, we thought we knew it all. We made some really immature decisions, especially with finances, and paid the consequences for them, over and over. Our differences, which are huge (he's an introvert, I'm an extrovert—complete opposites in every area), began to come into play. With me pregnant, finance problems, a toddler, and our differences, the stress began to build (i.e., the storms of life). Then all the unresolved issues of life started floating to the top. Of course, we didn't know we had unresolved issues at the time. Brad's way of dealing with things was to not deal with them, and my way was to try to control everything and get angry. Brad wanted to forget about it, and I wanted to fight about it. In the middle of all that came two innocent little boys who many times ended up being the scapegoat for my anger. For many years, Bradley and Robert suffered the consequences of my fury. Most of the time they really hadn't done anything that bad. They were typical little boys who did typical things. But because I expected perfection, they were never good enough.

Parenting is the hardest job in the world. Most people get no training, so they tend to do the only things they know—what was done to them. We can try to do things correctly, but when the stress gets high, we automatically fall into what we have learned from past experiences. It would be a lot easier to be a good parent if this wonderful, little instruction book came out with the baby when he was born and it gave all the specifics of how to raise this particular child. But that doesn't happen. Yes, we have the Bible, and many Christians will tell you that everything you need to know in life is found in the Bible, and that is true. But the Bible is a general overview. It gives us principles to follow.

As parents, we need specifics. For example, the Bible tells us in Proverbs 22:6, to

"Train a child in the way he should go, and when he is old he will not turn from it."

That is a wonderful principle, but how? How do we *"train a child in the way he should go,"* and what does that really mean? I thought, since I was a Christian and I was raising my children in church, that I was *"training my children in the way he should go."* It wasn't until my boys were almost raised that I learned that there are a lot of other specifics to that verse that I had no understanding of. Many people, like myself, never seek outside help to learn how to be good parents. I didn't even know there were places to get parent training. The only thing I had ever heard was that some professional was telling everybody it was bad to spank your child. I thought that was the dumbest thing I ever heard. How in the world could you raise a child without spanking them? I had always heard that the Bible says if you spare the rod you will spoil the child (I will be more specific about the rod later). I thought that meant that the more you spanked them, the less they would be spoiled, and I surely did not want a spoiled child. So I spanked—a lot! I spanked for everything, all the time. I spanked, slapped, hit, slugged, and screamed. I did whatever I needed to do to get my way as the parent.

As parents, we have a tendency to cycle parenting skills. I was raised in a time that children were to be seen and not heard. You weren't allowed to question what your parents did or said, and if you tried, there was punishment. Parents didn't ask your opinion. You weren't allowed to express emotions, especially anger. If you got angry at your parents about something, you held it in as long as you could, then went in your room with the door shut and cried. There was no question about spanking. That was the way to raise a child right. The concept of child abuse was practically nonexistent. The only child abuse was extremities like a child living in filth who was not cared for, fed, bathed, etc., or was abandoned. There was no outside agency butting their noses into family business. You did what you needed to do as the parent to get your child to behave. When Oklahoma became a state, there was a law that stated that if you killed a child as a result of punishment, it wasn't a crime. Laws weren't that extreme when I was a kid, but there was a freedom in parenting that is almost nonexistent today. Parents raised their kids the way they were raised, no questions asked.

Taking a mindset like this, and an angry parent, you can end up with some messed up kids. With no understanding of ADD, and having an angry dad, you can probably see why I ended up an angry adult. Therefore, I instilled within my boys that same anger. I never allowed them to express their anger when they were children, so now, as adults they have done so in inappropriate ways. I remember when Bradley was young, I would yell and scream at him, and he would say things like, *"Mama! Why do you always have to yell?"* He hated me yelling at him. If he tried to yell back at me, I would punish him. But Bradley and I had a tendency to butt heads (he was just like me), so he would yell back anyway then get punished.

If I was to pick the one thing that I think Bradley hated the most as a child, it would be that I yelled at him all the time. He didn't care about the spankings. He would tighten up his little butt cheeks and act tough. But he absolutely hated it when I yelled. And I did—all the time. Now when I hear him yelling at his wife or children, I try to remind him of how bad he hated that when he was a kid. Robert was different. He knew not to argue back. He was more like his daddy. He wouldn't say anything. Sometimes he would say things like, "*When is Bradley going to learn that he should just keep his mouth shut? If he wouldn't say anything, he wouldn't get in trouble.*" (Bradley was too headstrong for that.) I thought Robert was really smart. He knew when to keep his mouth shut, so he didn't get in near as much trouble as Bradley did. What I didn't understand was, because Robert didn't express his anger, he became a stuffer. He was like a volcano that keeps building up pressure on the inside until it can't handle the pressure any longer, and it erupts.

I remember the first time Robert blew up at me. He was a teenager, and Brad and I were yelling at him about a grade on his report card. He lost it. Brad and I were in such shock that we just looked at each other and didn't say a thing. I think that was the first time I realized how much Robert was becoming like his father. I told Brad that, and we laughed a little but didn't think much more about it. It wasn't until much later that we learned the consequences of us not dealing with Robert's anger. After he got married and moved out from under my control, Robert went into a constant stage of anger. When he was finally allowed to express what he had stuffed for so many years, he let it all go, at everything, all the time. He became violent and started hitting things like walls and doors, practically destroying his house. I am so thankful that because I recognized how wrong I was as a parent, I worked at repairing the hurts I had caused in my boys. From the time I started learning about my anger and how inappropriate I had been as a parent, I began working to repair our relationship. That has given me the opportunity to be able to speak to my sons about their anger and suggest they get help before they do to their children what I did to mine. You see, because I worked at mending that relationship, the door was open for me to talk to them.

Many times as parents, we can see the things our kids are doing wrong with our grandchildren, but if there isn't a good relationship, words that are meant to help can cause more hurts. I remember when my boys were small and my dad would tell me I was hitting them too much. In my mind, I couldn't imagine why he would say such a thing because I was only doing what he had taught me to do, which in turn was what his mom had taught him. So the cycle continues, unless we get help.

Without help, changing our ways of parenting is almost impossible. We will either do what our parents did, or we will determine to never do what our parents did. Either is usually an extreme. Without making this chapter a book within itself, I would like to share some basic principles of dealing with anger issues as a parent. These are principles that are easily understood and applicable.

Kids, like adults, have their own stress. They have parents, teachers, and peers to please, their own wants and needs, and their parents' problems that they overhear, to deal with. Even the best parents with the best intentions will share things kids don't need to hear. (This can cause a child to become parentified. A parentified child is one who tends to talk, act, and/or worry, like the parent instead of a child.)

Children, in their own little world, experience stress that many times is worse on their level than the stress we struggle with as adults. Then, we take our stress out on them. Kids come home after a day at school with their own problems, and then we come home and take our problems out on them, never considering that they already have enough of their own. The difference between the kids and us is, the kids don't have a choice. If a kid starts taking their anger out on a parent, the parent can either stop them or punish them if they don't stop. When a parent comes home and takes their anger out on the kid, the kid can't make the parent stop—they just have to take it. Think about this: how would you feel if you worked for a boss who constantly yelled in your face, embarrassed you in front of peers, called you stupid (or something worse), and basically showed you absolutely no respect? Most of us would quit the job. And those of us, who for some reason couldn't quit, would just be miserable. We don't even like being around people like that, much less working for them. Now, think of a child who lives with a parent who is like that. They can't just quit. They have to live with it. Is that fair?

Allow your children to express the way they are feeling, and then validate their emotions. If they are hurting, say something like, "*I'm sorry you are feeling hurt right now,*" or, "*I know that must hurt and I am really sorry.*" Let them know that their feelings are all right and that you care about them. When they are angry, teach them appropriate ways to deal with their anger instead of making them stuff it. And don't get angry just because they are angry. Teach them some of the principles taught in this, and many other good anger management books. There are quite a few written that are directed toward adolescents and teens. Teach them how to express feelings in appropriate ways, and to take ownership of those feelings by using "*I*" statements instead of "*you*" statements. Sometimes kids get upset when they do something wrong. Let them express their feelings and validate them, then discuss punishment. Don't punish, then discuss. That makes the punishment more important than the discussion or the validation of their feelings.

One of the biggest mistakes I made as a parent with a problem of being a perfectionist was that I never gave my kids a break. It didn't matter what area of life it was, I wanted them to do whatever they did perfectly. I was teaching a parenting class one evening when a parent asked me a question about chores. All of a sudden, in the middle of my answer, God gave me this eye-opening knowledge that just about knocked me over.

When I assigned chores to my sons, I did not accept the job they did unless it was perfect. The funny thing was, I gave myself breaks. Sometimes when I cleaned the kitchen, I would take everything off the counters and scrub them clean. But, more times than not, I would wipe off the center of the counters and leave it at that. But, oh my gosh! If one of the boys didn't get every spot clean in their bathroom, I would make them clean the whole thing again. Then the fights would start and so would the screaming. The same thing happened with vacuuming. Sometimes I would go around the edges against the baseboards, but most of the time I wouldn't. But they had to every time. Kids are kids, and they need to live lives of kids, not adults. When we expect our children to do things the way an adult does, we are setting ourselves, and our children, up for failure.

The final topic I want to discuss is the one I get asked the most about, and that is discipline. Many people believe that discipline is punishment, but the word discipline means to teach or guide. Discipline includes punishment and reward. It involves spending time talking to your children about rights and wrongs and what is expected of them, instead of just punishing them for doing wrong. The rod I mentioned earlier that the Bible talks about has been totally taken out of context. Shepherds used the rod in biblical times to guide a stray sheep back to the flock. They didn't use it to beat the sheep to death.

Today, it is against the law in many states to hit your child. Other states have laws that allow for spankings only if they are on the bottom and they don't leave marks. Anything outside those guidelines is against the law. I have had many clients who have been court ordered to take parenting classes, anger management, and to get counseling, as a result of Child Protective Services' involvement in their lives. Sometimes it was because the parent did something such as slap a kid in front of a teacher or spank a kid on the bottom and leave a mark. With the rising statistics of child abuse, states are coming down hard on parents to learn better ways of discipline than hitting. Too many people do not know how to draw the line between punishment and abuse. And, as I said before, many people do what their parents did to them, and that wasn't considered abuse. I have had clients who, when asked if they were abused as a child would answer no, but when asked how they were punished they reported things like being beaten with an extension cord. Because there is such a difference in beliefs about punishment, I will give you some basic guidelines to use when disciplining your children.

Discipline your kids because you want to teach them the difference between wrong and right. Never discipline because you are concerned about what others' might think. That is what I did. Whenever my boys did something wrong, my first thought was about what others would think of me as a parent. I would punish out of embarrassment. I would punish because I was concerned that if people thought I wasn't a good parent, they would reject me (of course, I did not understand that at the time). The real purpose for disciplining children is outlined for us in the scripture I mentioned at the first of this chapter. Proverbs 22:6, says to *"Train a child in the way he should go, and when he is old he will not turn from it."* There is a perfect explanation for discipline. If we discipline our children correctly, by biblical standards, when they are young, they will remember and apply those things as adults.

Never spank when you are angry. If your child has done something wrong and you feel your anger rising, take a time-out. This is a time for you and your child to individually self-talk about what happened and what would be the best punishment. It is a time for you to get your thoughts together and let your anger settle before punishing. Parents who spank when they are angry have more of a tendency to abuse. Be sure you know what your state law is before you decide it is okay to spank. I have heard stories of people who have gone to prison for spanking their child in public places where it was against the law to do so. Remember, the Bible says to obey the laws of the land[1]. Is it worth the risk of losing a child temporarily, or even permanently, for spanking, when other methods are available?

Make sure the punishment fits the crime. Young children are only able to comprehend short amounts of punishment time. For example, a three-year-old should be put in time-out for no longer than three minutes. A one-minute punishment for each year in age they are. Don't hit a kid when a simple discussion or time-out would have been sufficient for what they did. My only punishment was hitting, so my kids got hit for everything. I did not know about alternative ways to discipline my children.

One of the hardest things for a parent to do is be consistent. I was guilty of being inconsistent. I would tell the boys that if they did something one more time I would not let them go on the school trip the next day. But I would never stick to what I said. I didn't want my kids to miss out on the fun, so I would allow them to go. I would tell them they were grounded for the rest of their lives. Now, is that realistic? We should never threaten with a punishment we are not willing or able to follow through with. When you set rules, stick to them. Don't alter or let them slip later because it is harder to enforce them than it would be not to. Consistency is very difficult. It takes hard work and commitment. When you are tired, it is easier not to stick to the rules or to let the rules slide because it takes effort to follow through with the discipline. Proverbs 23:13–14 says,

"Do not withhold discipline from a child; if you punish him with the rod, he will not die. Punish him with the rod and save his soul from death."

Now, remember, the rod is used to teach or guide, not necessarily to spank.

Sometimes we don't want to discipline our children because we don't want them to hate us and we don't want them to think we are mean. Many parents, because of the way they were raised, want their children to be their best friends, so the line between being the parent and being child becomes blurred (again, parentification). There should be a difference in a relationship between two friends and the parent-child relationship. There are many scriptures in the Bible that instruct parents to discipline their children, and that children should honor and obey their parents. Those scriptures do not support the best friend theory.

Another reason we don't want to follow through with discipline is because the enemy makes us feel guilty when we do. He will start putting those thoughts in our heads, You are being just like your parents were. You don't love your kids. Now they are going to be mad at you. They won't like you anymore. And on and on. If we don't recognize the enemy's voice, rebuke it, and self-talk ourselves though those situations, we will never discipline our children. Read what this scripture says:

The watchman opens the gate for him, and the sheep listen to his voice. He calls his own sheep by name and leads them out. When he has brought out all his own, he goes on ahead of them, and his sheep follow him because they know his voice. But they will never follow a stranger; in fact, they will run away from him because they do not recognize a stranger's voice.
John 10:3–5

I believe the Lord is telling us in this scripture that not only can we hear His voice, but also we will run away from the voice of the enemy. This is a good scripture to confess about yourself, saying, "*I will hear and obey the voice of my Father, and I will run from the voice of the enemy.*" Then, when the enemy starts speaking lies to you, you will be able to recognize and overcome those things.

A parent who is inconsistent is a lazy parent. These parents are in essence telling the child that they can do anything they want because they are not going to follow through with the punishment. When we are inconsistent with punishment, we are opening more avenues for anger. We get angry at ourselves for not following through, and then we (or at least I did) somehow find a way to blame the kid.

During school, I learned a very effective concept to help me be consistent with discipline, but I didn't learn it until Robert was in high school. By then it was too late to use with Bradley. That concept was to write things down. I purchased an inexpensive spiral notebook for Robert to begin writing down different things I told him. Probably the biggest problem I had with my boys when it came to chores was that I would tell them to do something by a specific time and they would not do it. Then, when I would confront them about it, they would say that wasn't what I said. We could argue for hours about what I did or didn't say, and I, or we, would get angry and begin to express that anger in inappropriate ways.

The notebook completely changed that. Whenever I got to the point of feeling anger rise in me because Robert hadn't done something I told him to do, I would have him get out his notebook. I would make him write down word for word what I told him. I would also make him write out what the punishment would be if he didn't do it by a certain time. For example, he would write that he had until Sunday night at 10:00 to get his bathroom cleaned. If it wasn't done, I would take the keys to his car for a week, and he would have to ride the bus back and forth to school. He would have to sign and date it. He absolutely hated doing this, but it worked. Once we started using the notebook, I never had to take his keys from him. After we started writing thing down, our fights nearly ceased. It was incredible. I wish I would have learned that concept earlier, and I wish I wouldn't have waited until I was angry to use it. I truly believe that would have totally changed my relationship with my sons during their teenage years.

Notebooks work well for older kids, but for younger ones, chore and rule charts are more effective. Not only will they serve as a reminder of what the child's responsibilities are, but they will also help you and them establish punishment and rewards. I was thinking about kids one day and how, as parents, we make every decision for them when they are young. We decide things like who they can play with, where they are allowed to go, and what clothes they wear. Then, when they get their driver's licenses, we give them the keys to the car and expect them to make all the right decisions. The truth is, they have made very few decisions on their own before turning sixteen. Most kids never learn how to make decisions based on possible consequences until they are thrown into it. We are setting ourselves, and them, up for failure by doing this. Therefore, there is more of the chance of arguments and anger. And in my experience, the driving age is when this tends to gets worse.

You can establish chore and rule charts when your children are pretty young. My three-year-old grandsons understand that if they do something naughty, they will get punished. Once they are mature enough to comprehend this, you can begin doing charts with them. The older they get, the more involved they should get.

With toddlers, you can give them pennies in their bank or stars on a chart when they have accomplished good things (like picking up their toys or going to the bathroom in the potty). Time-outs and no movies work well for punishments.

As they mature, you can allow your child to help make decisions about the rewards when they do good and the punishments for when they are naughty. Kids can come up with some pretty good, and original, ideas for punishments and rewards in advance (before they are actually in trouble, etc.). I believe points charts are the most effective. Let's say they have ten chores they are to do each week and each chore is worth a maximum of ten points each. Write the chores down in list form, then the dates across the top of the chart, each having its own column. Then in the bottom corner, write a number below one hundred (ten chores times ten points equals one hundred points) that allows for compromise—let's say seventy-five. For each chore they do, based on how well they do the job, they are given a score from one to ten. If at the end of the week, they have reached at least seventy-five, they are given a predetermined reward. Some children, especially ones with ADD, cannot understand the concept of waiting a week for the reward, so they will need a daily reward.

Rewards do not have to be something purchased, although they can be if it is affordable. This is a good way to do weekly allowance. A nonmonetary weekly reward could be a friend spending the night, a trip to McDonald's play land, or a fun family game night. Daily rewards could be something like an hour playing a video game or getting to watch their choice of a TV show or video that evening. If the child does not reach seventy-five, then they will receive the pre-established punishment. The punishments can be the same thing as the reward, just minus it instead of plus (no playing outside, no games, no TV, etc.). If the child is really naughty, there can be alternate punishments such as groundings for the weekend, no video games for a certain amount of time, or something being taken away (like a bike) for a certain amount of time.

This will basically take the responsibility of decision making off your shoulders and onto theirs. They will make their decisions based on the punishments and rewards established. When they try to complain or argue, you only have to remind them that they are the ones who helped establish the charts and they chose the punishment/reward. The decision was in their hands, not yours, so you are not responsible for their decisions. I have seen the anger level in homes drastically reduce as a result of implementing this type of system in a family.

I have heard some really creative things parents have done with their children. One time, a parent told me she put some extra credit chores on sticky notes next to the chore chart. Her child could choose if she wanted to do the extra credit or not. They had a special reward for her if she earned over a certain score by using the extra credits. Also, the extra credit could be used to make up points when she had a bad day. This can become a fun family thing to do and very effective at reducing the number of arguments. Plus, it is teaching the child how to make decisions based on consequences, positive or negative. This same type of chart can also be made for house rules. For example, a child would receive so many points if they broke a rule. Then, if at the end of the week they had over a predetermined score, they would receive the predetermined punishment. Same with rewards. This would have stopped my spanking for everything.

Again, I want to say that parenting is the hardest job in the world. Most people get less training at being a parent than they do driving a car. There are no perfect parents; we can all use help. Parenting has a lot to do with trial and error. You try something a few times and if that doesn't work, instead of fighting, yelling, and screaming, because things aren't going the way you want, change what you are doing. Try something new. Be creative. Keep trying new things until you find something that works. And be consistent. Children will never learn without consistency.

There are many excellent resources available for parents today. Find some good parenting books to read or videos to watch. Choose authors who you know and trust. If you don't know any good authors, ask your pastor or someone you trust in your church. Go to the Christian bookstore to see what is available. Many times, the books available in the stores are also available to check out from the library. See if there is an agency in your community that offers parenting classes. Talk to people who have raised kids and ask them what worked. Look to the elders of your church. Not elders as in a position but with age. There are some really cool older people in our world that would love the opportunity to help a younger couple learn appropriate parenting skills that are adjusted for you and your family. If you can't find any of the things I have mentioned, pray. Ask God for wisdom and guidance in finding help. It is out there, you just have to seek it. You will be incredibly surprised at how learning a few positive parenting skills can help you get your anger under control.

CHAPTER 15
Taking Time-Outs

Romans 12:9 says,

"Love must be sincere. Hate what is evil; cling to what is good."

Controlling anger, before it controls you, is putting this verse into effect. We do hurtful things to the people we love when we use inappropriate anger. Shouldn't we hate that enough to want to change it? Cling to learning how to get your anger under control, no matter how difficult it is. Then you can show a sincere love to those you have previously treated ugly as a result of not being able to manage your anger. Time-outs are about getting your anger under control before it reaches the point of no return. Time-outs avoid and/or disrupt anger. The first thing to do is recognize what your anger triggers are. Here is a partial list of possible triggers: disappointments, someone trying to control you, incompetence or ignorance, failure, blame, injustice, abuse, embarrassment, frustration, guilt, mistakes, rejection, confusion, fear, jealousy, condemnation, depression, anxiety, hurt, and feelings of being overwhelmed. Ask yourself the following questions and write down your answers. What do I get angry about? Under what circumstance am I more apt to become angry? When am I the angriest?

    I can now look back and see how I would have answered those questions. I hated it if someone tried to control me. When someone tried to control me, I wouldn't let them know how much it bothered me, but I would take the anger out on someone close to me like my kids or husband. Some people don't mind being controlled by others. I am too headstrong for that. I want to do things my way. I want to be the one in control. This is one of the reasons many parents and teenagers continually fight. Teenagers are going through their stage of trying to figure out who they are. They want independence. When their parents try to control them, they rebel. This is why Bradley (my oldest son) and I butted heads so much. We have very similar personalities, and when I wanted my way, and he wanted his way, a fight would commence. He would want to go hang out with his buddies, but I wanted his room cleaned first. He would argue that he could do it when he got home. I wanted it done right then. He would get so angry with me when I forced him to do something he didn't like or kept him from doing something he wanted to do.

    As I have already said, rejection was also a huge issue for me. I would get angry when I felt rejected. That is why I did so many things to try to prevent rejection. When I was a kid, I never felt like what I did was good enough. My older sister was perfect, and I was the failure. Even teachers would ask me why I couldn't be more like my sister. I would resent it when people would say that. Because of the ADD, I felt rejected all the time.

When I became an adult, I didn't want to feel rejected anymore. That's why I became "*perfect.*" Whenever I felt rejected, I would express anger instead of hurt. Then I would take it out on those close to me.

Stress was also one of my major triggers. When I became stressed about whatever difficulties of life I was facing, I couldn't handle all the internal pressure. So I would explode, again at those I loved. The littlest thing could set me off, and I would make a major deal out of it. One of the boys could accidentally spill something, and I would instantly get angry. I would get offended at something someone said or did, and many times I would take things totally out of the concept in which they were meant. This was even worse if it happened to be a time when I was dealing with PMS.

Today, I still struggle with handling seemingly insignificant circumstances when my stress level is high. I am really thankful I learned how to take time-outs. I have learned to not even try to deal with difficult circumstances if I have been sick, if I haven't gotten enough sleep, if I am feeling anxious or nervous about something, or if I am already upset about something else. I avoid those things so I can avoid getting angry. Avoidance is a time-out because you allow yourself time to feel better before you encounter difficult circumstances.

Remember in Chapter 8, when I suggested you pay attention to how your body changes physically when you begin to get angry? Some examples of body changes are sweaty palms, upset stomach, headache or head throbbing, shaking, rapid heartbeat, knees knocking, and/or gripping fists. These are called somatic complaints. The next step in taking time-outs is learning how your body changes when you begin to get angry. Once you can recognize your somatic complaints, you can stop yourself before the anger escalates. The next time you get angry, try to identify how you are feeling. It might help if you make a list of your body changes. Writing them down makes them visual and therefore can help them be easier for you to identify when they begin. The more senses you are able to utilize, the better you will be able to recognize them and learn how to stop what you are doing when they begin.

When you are in a discussion with someone and you begin to feel your body changes taking place, tell them you want to take a time out. It is important that you don't just walk away without saying something first. That is disrespectful, and it promotes anger in the other person. It is also necessary to express it in a nice way, and you should remember to take ownership of your feelings. Don't blame them for your need to take a time out. When you say, "*I want to take a time out,*" you are letting the other person know that you are feeling anger rise in you and you need some time alone before you do something inappropriate. It would be a good idea to discuss time-outs in advance with people you are close to before you try using them.

When I first started learning about time-outs, I decided to take one when an argument Brad and I were in began to escalate. He started raising his voice at me and I felt myself getting angry, so I walked into our room, shut the door, and lay on the bed. About a minute later, Brad kicked the door open and started yelling at me at the top of his lungs to never do that to him again. Remember, this was coming from a man who hardly ever lost his temper. I was in such shock that I just laid their there looking at him. I didn't say a word. I had never seen him that angry. I didn't realize that I needed to tell him what I was doing before I took a time out. As a result, he felt disrespected and therefore became very angry. As you can imagine, I learned an important lesson, and I never did that again.

Now is the time to talk about the fun part of taking time-outs. Time-outs are for you to calm down, relax, and self-talk. You need to get into an environment where that is possible. First, make a list of things you enjoy doing. Doing the things you have listed will help you calm down. They can help you take your mind off the situation long enough to relax. My favorite thing to do when I am upset is to take a long, hot bath. Sometimes I light a candle and play soft worship music. I try to focus on something other than what I am upset about. I listen to the music and watch the flame on the candle flicker. Then, after I am totally relaxed, I begin to self-talk. I try to figure out why I was getting upset—the root cause. I begin to ask myself questions. Was there another emotion I was covering with my anger? Is this topic serious enough to get into a heated argument about? Am I really upset about this particular thing, or are there other triggering forces like stress, lack of sleep, or illness that are making this situation feel worse than it really is? Who am I upset at? Who is the person I'm arguing with? What do I know about them and the condition of their heart? I begin to work on a solution instead of focusing on how angry I am at what they did or said.

As I begin to self-talk through these type questions and the answers to them, I can begin to see the situation from another perspective. I can then formulate in my mind what the best way to handle it is without getting angry. When I go back to continue the discussion, I have a clearer mind, and I am prepared to act instead of react. One important thing I have to remember is that I need to keep my self-talk in the positive. The enemy will try to put negative thoughts in my head, and I could possibly take ownership of them and focus on them instead of a positive solution. I need to recognize and rebuke those negative thoughts before they get out of hand. I never want the enemy to have control over me and my anger. (See the Chapter on Thoughts.)

Here is a list of things you can do during your time out. This list in no way is exhaustive, it is just to give you some ideas, so you can use them to develop your own.

- Take a walk.
- Exercise.
- Play a sport (i.e., basketball by yourself).
- Play a video game.
- Watch a funny TV show.
- Read.
- Listen to relaxing music or a tape on relaxing.
- Draw.
- Pray.
- Get outside. Get a breath of fresh air.
- Ride a bike or motorcycle. (one of my personal favorites)
- Find someone you trust to talk to.
- Someone who will hold you accountable instead of joining your pity party.
- Take a nap.
- Journal.
- Do something on your computer; get online.
- Clean or do yard work.
- Go for a drive.
- Go shopping (if you have money, otherwise it might make the situation worse).

Again, it is important to list the things you personally enjoy. Some of these things might make your situation worse instead of better. It may take several times of trial and error before you figure out what works best for you.

One time when I was teaching an anger management class, I had a brilliant idea. When you take your time out, go to the freezer and get a piece of ice. You can rub it on your face and arms. A piece of ice can be a quick reminder that you need to *"chill out"* or *"cool off."*

Another thing I thought would be interesting was to go look at yourself in the mirror. Humor can be one of the best diffusers of anger. Have you ever looked at yourself when you are angry? Sometimes it can be quite comical. If you can laugh at yourself, you can calm yourself down.

Going on an imaginary trip is also a good way to calm down and take your focus off the current circumstance. Find somewhere quiet and comfortable where you know you won't be interrupted. Then close your eyes, and imagine you are either at one of your favorite places or somewhere you would love to go. See how clear you can focus on where you are. Smell the smells, hear the noises, see the beauty, and relax.

The sound of water can be very soothing. If you don't have some type of a waterfall or a noisemaker, purchase one. They can be very inexpensive and well worth the money. Sit next to it, close your eyes, and focus on the sounds. Smells can also be soothing. Purchase a candle that is your favorite smell. Burn it while you are listening to the sounds. This will use two of your senses, which will help calm you even more.

Learn how to relax. There are numerous books on the market that teach relaxation skills. Here is the easiest one I know about. Again, go somewhere quiet where you won't be disturbed. You can play some soothing music, or start a noisemaker like the waterfall. Lay down flat on your back, and close your eyes. To recognize the tenseness, and then relaxation of your muscles, tighten your hands into a fist as tight as you can and hold it for about ten seconds. Then relax them. Do this a few times so you can recognize the feeling. Then, beginning at your toes, tighten and relax every muscle in your body. Keep your total focus on the part of the body you are trying to relax. Do your toes, feet, ankles, calves, knees, thighs, hips, etc., until you have relaxed every muscle you can like this. While you are doing this, take long, deep breaths. Believe it or not, you can even relax your eyes, nose, and ears this way.

When you are in a totally relaxed state, let your imagination wander. You can do as previously stated and go on an imaginary trip, or listen to the music or the noise you have been playing. Stay there as long as you can. You may even fall asleep, which isn't necessarily a bad thing. You will wake up more relaxed. By the way, if you have trouble falling asleep at night, this relaxation technique might help. After you have relaxed, remember to self-talk before you go back to the discussion that you became upset about. If you don't, the time out will be wasted time.

I have read and heard many discussions about how long a time-out should be. I don't think I can set a perfect time out time for you because each person is different. What might take one person an hour or so to do, another person might be able to do in several minutes. The depth of your anger is also a determining factor when trying to figure out how much time you should take. You may want to determine the length of your time-out based on each individual circumstance. If you only allow yourself thirty minutes, but you aren't really ready to face the situation in a healthy manner, you could go right back into the same situation you left.

CHAPTER 16
Additional Topics

In this chapter, I would like to highlight a few issues that are worth discussing that don't require a whole chapter to do so, or would take another whole book to discuss in detail. I would like to start out with a list of common anger triggers. Although I have mentioned quite a few throughout this book, I would like to give you a more extensive list that you can later refer to when you find yourself getting angry.

Manipulation: Are you angry because you are trying to manipulate someone and it's not working? An example of this would be moping around the house to get attention instead of directly addressing the issue. Or have you realized that someone is trying to manipulate you and you don't like it? An example of this would be a teenager trying to get his/her way by sweet-talking or doing extra chores without being asked. Please don't get me wrong here. It would be great if your teenager decided to help out and do extras without being asked. But if it is done for manipulation, it is wrong. Have you ever read the story in the Bible of Esther? It is a story about an evil man named Haman who tries to manipulate a situation for his good instead of the good of the people. Esther 9:25 tells us the reward Haman received for his evil deed.

"But when the plot came to the king's attention, he issued written orders that the evil scheme Haman had devised against the Jews should come back onto his own head, and that he and his sons should be hanged on the gallows."

I think *"evil scheme"* is a very good description for manipulation.

Control of others or situations: Control is much like manipulation. The difference is that manipulation is usually more passive, done in secret. Control, on the other hand, is usually done with more bold, obvious actions. Are you angry because you are trying to control someone who is not allowing you to do so? Or are you angry because you feel like you are losing control of something and you don't know how to get a handle on it? When we are trying to control, we are not trusting God. The Bible tells us in Proverbs 3:5–6 to, *"Trust in the LORD with all your heart and lean not on your own understanding; in all your ways acknowledge Him, and He will make your paths straight."* The more we learn to trust God, the more we will be able to let go of control issues. This takes self-talk and lots of prayer!

Someone controlling you: Joshua 24:15b says, *"But as for me and my household, we will serve the LORD."* Make a decision that you will not serve man, only God. If someone gets angry because you will not serve him, then let him get angry. Serving anyone through control is sin. I'm not talking about having a servant's heart, like Jesus showed us through His example (John 13:3-17). When you allow someone else to control you, there is no room left for the work of the Holy Spirit. He can't work where someone else is in control.

Guilt (or shame): Are you actually feeling guilty about something you have done wrong, but are covering up the guilt with anger? Allow the Holy Spirit to convict you to repentance and change, but rebuke the guilt that comes from the enemy. Allow yourself to be humbled. Proverbs 18:12 tells us that, *"Before his downfall a man's heart is proud, but humility comes before honor."* Sometimes it is hard to admit you are wrong, but humility is a good thing.

The need to be right: Do you get angry when someone doubts you or you feel like they think you are wrong when you know you are right? The need to be right stems from the fear of rejection. In reality, it doesn't matter if others think you are right or not. What matters is what you know in your heart, and what you know, God knows.

Defensiveness: Are you angry because you feel someone put you on the defense? Did they attack you with words or attitudes? Or did someone accuse you of doing something you didn't do? Did they address a situation beginning with *"You..."*? If this is causing your anger, then it is time to self-talk. You can respond to harshness with niceness. Proverbs 16:24 says, *"Pleasant words are a honeycomb, sweet to the soul and healing to the bones."* Responding to someone who has spoken harshly to you with pleasant words could help them to calm down.

Self-pity: Are you feeling sorry for yourself? Are you trying to have a pity party but can't find anyone to join you? Are you responding to your *"self"* feelings with anger toward others? Many times we feel sorry for ourselves and want others to feel sorry for us. Maybe things really aren't fair.

Commit your way to the LORD; trust in Him and He will do this: He will make your righteousness shine like the dawn, the justice of your cause like the noonday sun. Be still before the LORD and wait patiently for Him; do not fret when men succeed in their ways, when they carry out their wicked schemes. Refrain from anger and turn from wrath; do not fret—it leads only to evil. For evil men will be cut off, but those who hope in the LORD will inherit the land.

Psalm 37:5–9

Trying to get attention: Is your outburst of anger just a scheme to get attention? Are you feeling insecure, unimportant, insignificant, and/or unnoticed? Stop yourself before it gets out of hand. Begin to confess the scriptures that tell you who God says you are. List some of your good qualities to yourself. Fight off those fiery darts of the enemy as it says in Ephesians, *"take up the shield of faith, with which you can extinguish all the flaming arrows of the evil one"* (6:16).

Getting even: Are you trying to get even with someone for something they have done to you and are you doing so with inappropriate outbursts of anger? Romans 12:20–21 says, *"If your enemy is hungry, feed him; if he is thirsty, give him something to drink. In doing this, you will heap burning coals on his head. Do not be overcome by evil, but overcome evil with good."* Here are a couple of examples. When you have a lousy waitress, give her a big tip. If someone is being ugly to you, be nice back.

Jealousy or envy: Are you angry because someone is getting something you think you deserve? Or does it seem like everyone else is always getting blessed and you are not? Maybe this is a trial God is allowing you to go through. Seek Him to find out what He is wanting you to learn. *"Give, and it will be given to you. A good measure, pressed down, shaken together and running* *over, will be poured into your lap. For with the measure you use, it will be measured to you"* (Luke 6:38). Remember to do your part, and God will bless you. His timing is perfect.

Criticism: Are you angry because someone has criticized you? Even the best constructive criticism can sometimes be hard to take. Proverbs 4:13 tells us to *"Hold on to instruction, do not let it go; guard it well, for it is your life."* Take some time to think about what this person has said. Is there something of value in it? Keep that part. Throw the rest away. Many times things that initially hurt can cause great growth.

Power: Are your outbursts of anger your way of showing others what kind of power you have? This is one of the things I did. When I felt insecure, I would lash out in anger. Then no one could tell how insecure I was feeling. It was a good way to cover my real feelings. But remember, our true strength is in the Lord, not in what we can, or cannot do. *"It is God who arms me with strength and makes my way perfect"* (Psalm 18:32).

Embarrassment: Are you showing anger in place of embarrassment? This is one of the hardest emotions to overcome. No one likes to be embarrassed. When you are feeling embarrassed, pray and ask God to give you His peace instead of lashing out in anger. He gives us this promise in Psalm 29:11, *"The LORD gives strength to His people; the LORD blesses His people with peace."*

Delays: Are you in a hurry and some dummy is causing you delays? Take a few deep breaths. Think for a minute. Why are you in a hurry? Is it necessary? Is there something God wants you to do that if you hurry you might miss? Look around, survey the situation. There may be someone in your path that God wants you to minister to. Or He may be allowing things to block your way to prevent something evil that you are not aware of. I received this e-mail the other day and feel it appropriate to share it with you.

WHERE GOD WANTS ME—*One day I happened to call a man on business that I didn't know, have not—nor will probably ever talk to again. But this day, he felt like talking. He was head of security in New York City. His company had invited the remaining members of another company, whose office had been decimated by the September 11th attack on the Twin Towers, to share their office space. With his voice full of awe, he told me stories of why these people were alive and their counterparts were dead. All the stories were just little things. You might know about the head of the company who got in late that day because his son started kindergarten. Another fellow was alive because it was his turn to bring donuts. There were other stories that I hope and pray will someday be gathered and put in a book. The one that struck me was the man who put on a new pair of shoes that morning. He took the various means to get to work, but before he got there, he developed a blister on his foot. He stopped at a drugstore to buy a Band-Aid. That is why he is alive. Now when I am stuck in traffic, miss an elevator, turn back to answer a ringing telephone...all the little things that annoy me...I think to myself, this is exactly where God wants me to be at this very moment. May God continue to bless you with all those annoying little things.*

—Author Unknown

Hmmmm...gives you another aspect to consider when little delays get in the way. Who knows what God is up to?

Ignorance: One of my biggest irritations in life is ignorant people. I have to self-talk through so many circumstances where I am dealing with ignorance and feel impatience rise up in me. Impatience in me almost always gives rise to anger. Sometimes I just ask myself, "*What would Jesus do in this situation?*" The Bible is full of scriptures that tell us that as Christians, we should show patience. In Colossians 3:12, Paul tells us, "*Therefore, as God's chosen people, holy and dearly loved, clothe yourselves with compassion, kindness, humility, gentleness and patience.*" If I blow it during one of these times, what I have really blown is my Christian witness.

Humor: One thing I don't think I have talked about at all in this book is humor. Sometimes humor can be the best way to defuse anger. Proverbs 17:22 says, "*A cheerful heart is good medicine, but a crushed spirit dries up the bones.*" I talked a little about looking in the mirror when you are angry in the chapter on time-outs. Have you tried it? We can look pretty ridiculous when we are angry. Our faces get distorted, and we make some pretty hilarious expressions. When Brad and I were first married, every time I would get mad at him about something, he would get right in my face and smile really big. Then he would say, "*You can't be mad at me. You love me too much.*" His face would be so close to mine that it would look distorted as he spoke. I never could stay angry when he did that. I would just bust out laughing. It worked every time.

It doesn't matter how wrong one of my grandkids are, if they start smiling or laughing when I am getting on to them, I can't help but laugh. I wasn't that way with my own boys, but Brad was. If they did something funny when he was mad, he would just crack up at them. They knew they could get their daddy going. We would be sitting in a restaurant eating, and they would do something that embarrassed me. I would get so angry. Brad would be rolling in laughter. Then, of course, I would get angry at him too. I never knew how to relax and have a good time with the boys. Again, my perfection got in the way. I would stay angry and Brad would have a good time. I always had to be so serious, not realizing how healthy laughter is. If we can find something funny to do or say when the air is getting tense, it can help reduce the pressure. It doesn't mean that we have to forget the topic, but we can approach it with a better attitude when we allow ourselves to apply some humor to it.

Redirect your anger: Another good thing to do is to channel, or redirect, anger to something positive. Many people get angry when bad things happen, and then spend the rest of their lives angry about that situation. The mother who started M.A.D.D. (Mothers Against Drunk Drivers) channeled her anger about her child being killed by a drunk driver toward helping other parents who experience the same thing. This is especially helpful in cases of injustice. If something happens to you that you feel is injustice, see if you can figure out a way to help others who have had the same type of thing happen to them.

Writing: Writing is another good way to redirect anger. When something happens that you become angry about, sit down and write a letter. It can be to someone who is specifically involved in the situation, or just a letter about what happened. This isn't a letter that necessarily needs to be sent. It is a very good way to express and validate your own anger about a circumstance that you might otherwise do in an inappropriate way. I have written many letters. I have mailed very few. It just seems that I feel much better after writing my feelings down. It is a form of release. I have had many clients write letters to people from their past that hurt them. Then we discuss the letters during sessions. This helps them to let go of some of that past stuff. They get to say what they have always wanted to say but for one reason or another were not allowed to. Sometimes we catch the letters on fire and watch them burn. This is a significant way to let go. All those emotions that were stored up as a result of that event are burned up; they become ashes, and they are released. Tearing the letters up is also effective. The actual action of tearing releases some of the built up anger. Journaling or writing in a diary could have much the same effects as writing a letter.

Don't use drugs or alcohol: One of the biggest mistakes some people make when they get angry is to drink or take drugs. This is only a temporary fix. Eventually, the effects of the drugs or alcohol wear off, and the reality of the situation is still there. This is how many people become addicts. They keep taking the drugs or drinking to cover the pain. Each time the effects of what they are doing wear off, the feelings are still there. So they do more and more until they become addicted. Also, drinking and/or doing drugs can actually amplify the feelings of anger. As a result, the effects of the drug can give you a false feeling of power. Then you may do something you wouldn't normally do if you had a clear head. You may say or do things that are more hurtful than you already have as a result of your anger. Then, after the effects of the drug has worn off, the circumstances you have to face are more difficult than they were before you started drinking or taking the drugs.

Apologize: Another issue I have mentioned but not really discussed is apologies. We should apologize whether we are right or wrong. Then forgive. The Bible tells us if we want forgiveness, we have to first give it (Matthew 6:12). And it is never too late to apologize. As adults, how many of you would love for someone from your past who hurt you to come to you now and apologize? For many of us, that would be the ultimate freeing event to release us from past issues. If you can think of anything you have done in the past that hurt someone, go to them and apologize. Ask them to forgive you, especially if it is your children. Maybe while reading this book you have realized that you made some major mistakes as a parent. I believe that God takes those things that the enemy means for harm and turns them around for good (Genesis 50:20, Romans 8:28). If telling my story about the wrong I did to my family helps you to make things right with yours, then God has made some good out of what the enemy meant for harm. Go to your children and make things right. Just as you would love for someone to do that for you, so would they.

Domestic violence: I have not addressed the issue of domestic violence in this book for a reason. Domestic violence is a result of extreme uncontrolled anger and takes much more professional help than what I can offer in this book. If you are experiencing any type of domestic violence in your home, please seek professional help. I have never seen a case where someone prone to be violent has been able to stop without getting professional help.

Physical ailments: I have stated before that frequently our physical ailments are a direct result of our emotional struggles. As we allow God to heal our emotions, many of our physical healings will come naturally. What good would it do for God to heal our physical ailments, when our emotions are still a wreck? He would heal them, then all the emotional baggage we carry would cause the physical stuff to come right back. Countless lives are weighed down by the difficulties of life, the things the enemy has thrown at us, and the unfair circumstances we have had to face. This weight can become so heavy that we can mentally and physically break down, much like ice on the branches of a tree. God told Moses that He was Jehovah Rapha, the God who heals (Exodus 15:26). And the psalmist said God heals the brokenhearted and binds up their wounds (Psalm 147:3). That word "*heals*" in the original Hebrew means to mend by stitching. As a seamstress, I understand that when you stitch something back together, you have to do so one stitch at a time. Many times, God heals us in the same way. It is a process that can take time. But, there is a wonderful benefit to God's healing. When He stitches us back together, He includes a very special crimson cord that He weaves into every seam. This cord is made of the strongest, most durable material in heaven or earth. It is the blood of Jesus. Ecclesiastes 4:12 tells us, *"Though one may be overpowered, two can defend themselves. A cord of three strands is not quickly broken."*

Conclusion

Images of anger are embedded on our minds. They are like snapshots; our eyes, and ears, are the cameras. They can be very vivid: yelling, screaming, hitting, or hurting. They can pop into our minds at any time, without warning. Everyday things like watching a movie, something someone says, smells, sounds, and/or dreams can trigger these memories. They work like filters, which our thoughts and feelings pass through before we process. When these images are triggered, they can control us. They used to control me, but no longer. I control them. I choose how I will act when circumstances arise that have the potential for me to react in inappropriate and sinful ways. I choose. No one makes me act or feel a certain way. I have the tools and techniques to recognize anger-provoking situations and carefully think through, self-talk, how I am going to respond. Am I perfect? Absolutely not! Do I still make mistakes? Yes! Anger management is a lifelong process. Reading a book or going through a 17-week program does not instantly change years of bad habits and behaviors. I am very thankful that I have the opportunity to teach anger management on a continuing basis. It serves as a constant reminder to me. It keeps my mind refreshed of the tools and techniques I have learned and it helps me apply them appropriately. But most people do not have the opportunities I have. Not everyone can read this book and then start leading weekly anger management classes. However, there are many things you can do.

I would first suggest that if you have not done so already, go to my website, www.drteresadavis.com and purchase and download the corresponding workbook to this anger management book. Then take your time to work through each page, being as open and honest as possible. This workbook will cause you to dig deep and think about things you would rather forget. But it is only through healing, God's healing, that the pain of these memories will diminish, and therefore, cease to control you and the way you respond to anger provoking situations.

Another suggestion would be for you to find a Christian anger management program that you can participate in. Being with people who are experiencing the same problems and feelings you have can be very helpful, and encouraging. As you hear their stories you can relate to them. As they learn how to work through their anger issues, you learn also.

On occasion I run into old anger management clients who I have not seen in years. Many times they will tell me that they keep this book next to their beds so they can refer back to it as needed. They read and re-read, highlight and make notes in the margins. Some tell me how they have shared what they have learned with others. They have asked those they trust to serve as accountability partners for them. These are people they can call when they feel their anger is elevating and they trust them to talk them through instead of arguing or fighting with them. We very seldom see ourselves the way others see us. Therefore, having someone we trust to hold us accountable for our words and actions can be extremely helpful.

I think the anger management skill that has helped me the most is learning to control my thoughts. The Bible tells us in 2 Cor. 10:4-5 to bring every thought captive to the obedience of Christ. The more I learn to take all my thoughts to Christ, instead of instantly reacting to them, the better I am becoming at daily managing my anger. I am learning how not to immediately react to what I feel, but to examine the facts of the situation before I respond.

Early in 2009 I completed my doctorate degree in Pastoral and Community Counseling. For my dissertation, I did a study to find the effectiveness of my anger management program that includes the information printed on the pages of this book. The results of that study provided reliable evidence that this program is effective both for volunteer and court ordered clients. These results indicate that, for those who want to control their anger and will put forth the time and effort needed to do so, that the program works.

I have heard many people say that they have prayed and prayed for God to deliver them from anger. I do believe that God still performs instantaneous miracles. However, for most of us, it is a process. If God miraculously delivered us from anger, the next time an anger provoking situation happened, we would revert back to our old ways because we had not learned new coping skills. The Bible tells us in Phil. 1:6 that God will complete the work He has begun in us. A willing heart opens the door for God to work. Once we allow Him to begin the work, He will bring it to completion.

NOTES TO THE TEXT

INTRODUCTION

[1] Diagnostic and Statistical Manual of Mental Disorders, fourth edition, (DSM-IV), (American Psychiatric Association), 1994.

[2] Edward M. Hallowell, M.D., Driven To Distraction: Recognizing and Coping With Attention Deficit Disorder From Childhood Through Adulthood, (Touchstone), 1995.

CHAPTER 1

[1] 2 Cor 12:20—For I am afraid that when I come I may not find you as I want you to be, and you may not find me as you want me to be. I fear that there may be quarreling, jealousy, outbursts of anger, factions, slander, gossip, arrogance and disorder.

[2] Matt 5:23–24—Therefore, if you are offering your gift at the altar and there remember that your brother has something against you, leave your gift there in front of the altar. First go and be reconciled to your brother; then come and offer your gift.

CHAPTER 2

[1] 2 Cor 5:21—God made him who had no sin to be sin for us, so that in him we might become the righteousness of God.

[2] Phil 4:13—I can do everything through him who gives me strength.

³ Rom 8:28—And we know that in all things God works for the good of those who love him, who have been called according to his purpose.

⁴ John 10:10—The thief comes only to steal and kill and destroy; I have come that they may have life, and have it to the full.

⁵ Gal 3:26—You are all sons of God through faith in Christ Jesus.

⁶ Rom 8:37—No, in all these things we are more than conquerors through him who loved us.

CHAPTER 3

¹ Matt 13:38–39—The field is the world, and the good seed stands for the sons of the kingdom. The weeds are the sons of the evil one, and the enemy who sows them is the devil. The harvest is the end of the age, and the harvesters are angels.

² Eph 6:13–18—Therefore put on the full armor of God, so that when the day of evil comes, you may be able to stand your ground, and after you have done everything, to stand. Stand firm then, with the belt of truth buckled around your waist, with the breastplate of righteousness in place, and with your feet fitted with the readiness that comes from the gospel of peace. In addition to all this, take up the shield of faith, with which you can extinguish all the flaming arrows of the evil one. Take the helmet of salvation and the sword of the Spirit, which is the word of God. And pray in the Spirit on all occasions with all kinds of prayers and requests. With this in mind, be alert and always keep on praying for all the saints.

[3] Webster's Encyclopedia of Dictionaries, New American Edition, (Ottenheimer Publishers, Inc.), 1981.

[4] 2 Cor 12:9—And he said to me, My grace is sufficient for thee: for my strength is made perfect in weakness. Most gladly therefore will I rather glory in my infirmities, that the power of Christ may rest upon me (KJV).

[5] Acts 8:20—Peter answered: May your money perish with you, because you thought you could buy the gift of God with money!

CHAPTER 5

[1] Isa 53:3—He was despised and rejected by men, a man of sorrows, and familiar with suffering. Like one from whom men hide their faces he was despised, and we esteemed him not.

Mark 9:12—Jesus replied, To be sure, Elijah does come first, and restores all things. Why then is it written that the Son of Man must suffer much and be rejected?

Luke 9:22—And he said, The Son of Man must suffer many things and be rejected by the elders, chief priests and teachers of the law, and he must be killed and on the third day be raised to life.

Luke 17:25—But first he must suffer many things and be rejected by this generation.

CHAPTER 7

[1] Webster's Encyclopedia of Dictionaries, New American Edition, (Ottenheimer Publishers, Inc.), 1981.

CHAPTER 8

[1] Webster's Encyclopedia of Dictionaries, New American Edition, (Ottenheimer Publishers, Inc.), 1981.

[2] Isaiah 54:17—No weapon that is formed against thee shall prosper; and every tongue that shall rise against thee in judgment thou shalt condemn. This is the heritage of the servants of the Lord, and their righteousness is of me, saith the Lord (KJV).

[3] I John 4:4—You, dear children, are from God and have overcome them, because the one who is in you is greater than the one who is in the world.

[4] James 4:7—Submit yourselves, then, to God. Resist the devil, and he will flee from you.

[5] Rom 8:1—Therefore, there is now no condemnation for those who are in Christ Jesus.

[6] John 16:8—When he comes, he will convict the world of guilt in regard to sin and righteousness and judgment.

CHAPTER 10

[1] Eph 4:32—Be kind and compassionate to one another, forgiving each other, just as in Christ God forgave you.

CHAPTER 11

[1] Phil 3:14—I press on toward the goal to win the prize for which God has called me heavenward in Christ Jesus.

CHAPTER 12

¹ James 1:2–4—Consider it pure joy, my brothers, whenever you face trials of many kinds, because you know that the testing of your faith develops perseverance. Perseverance must finish its work so that you may be mature and complete, not lacking anything.

² Rom 8:28—And we know that in all things God works for the good of those who love him, who have been called according to his purpose.

³ 2 Th 3:3—But the Lord is faithful, and he will strengthen and protect you from the evil one.

⁴ Isa 54:17—no weapon forged against you will prevail, and you will refute every tongue that accuses you. This is the heritage of the servants of the LORD, and this is their vindication from me, declares the LORD.

⁵ Rom 4:17—As it is written: I have made you a father of many nations. He is our father in the sight of God, in whom he believed-- the God who gives life to the dead and calls things that are not as though they were.

⁶ 2 Cor 5:7—We live by faith, not by sight.

⁷ 2 Pet 1:3-4—His divine power has given us everything we need for life and godliness through our knowledge of him who called us by his own glory and goodness. Through these he has given us his very great and precious promises, so that through them you may participate in the divine nature and escape the corruption in the world caused by evil desires.

CHAPTER 13

[1] Ps 4:4—In your anger do not sin; when you are on your beds, search your hearts and be silent. Selah

Eph 4:26—In your anger do not sin. Do not let the sun go down while you are still angry.

CHAPTER 14

[1] Heb 13:17—Obey your leaders and submit to their authority. They keep watch over you as men who must give an account. Obey them so that their work will be a joy, not a burden, for that would be of no advantage to you.

Rom 13:1—Everyone must submit himself to the governing authorities, for there is no authority except that which God has established. The authorities that exist have been established by God.

www.ingramcontent.com/pod-product-compliance
Lightning Source LLC
LaVergne TN
LVHW051057080426
835508LV00019B/1933